ESSENTIALS OF

Comparative Government

Samuel A. Johnson, PH.D.

Professor of History and Government,
HARRIS TEACHERS COLLEGE
Lecturer in Political Science,
WASHINGTON UNIVERSITY
Former Lecturer in Government,
ST. LOUIS UNIVERSITY

BARRON'S EDUCATIONAL SERIES, INC.

WOODBURY, NEW YORK

THIS SURVEY OF COMPARATIVE GOVERNMENT undertakes to present, briefly and simply, comparisons of significant features of the governments of the major countries, along with some distinctive features of the governments of some of the less important countries. Every effort has been made to avoid technicalities and confusing details.

Instead of the traditional pattern of describing separately the government of each of several countries, each branch or aspect of government is taken up in a chapter or section, comparing this branch or aspect in various countries. This plan is intended to clarify comparisons better than the traditional plan.

Readers are cautioned to bear in mind that governments change from time to time, by constitutional amendment or otherwise. It is quite possible that some things stated in these pages may have changed by the time the book is used. It is well, too, in using books listed in the Bibliography for reference, to note the date of publication. Some books are included which, though out of date on some particulars, are still useful for other material.

This little book can stand alone as a simple text in comparative government, but it will also be useful to supplement a larger book of the traditional pattern by simplifying and clarifying comparisons. It is hoped, also, that many readers other than students will find it interesting and instructive.

I wish to express my gratitude to my wife, Winifred Feder Johnson, for her valuable assistance in the preparation of the manuscript.

Samuel A. Johnson
ST. LOUIS, MISSOURI

CONTENTS

ONE

Government in General

Meaning of Terms

WHAT IS GOVERNMENT? Government is a term which everyone understands, but which defies adequate definition. It is sometimes defined as "rulership," but that only adds to the vagueness. For our purpose, we may think of government as the organization which manages the affairs of a community, large or small, and conducts the relationships of that community with other communities. The community may be a country, a city, or anything in between. Thus, in the United States, we have the national government, fifty state governments, and an untold number of local governments. In comparative government we are concerned with comparing the governments of different countries or, to be more exact, the governments of sovereign states, but this calls for some definitions to clarify our terms.

SOVEREIGNTY. One term we shall meet again and again is sovereignty and its adjective form sovereign. Sovereignty is usually defined as supreme power. As applied to states, it has two aspects: internal and external. Within the state, sovereignty means complete right to rule. This does not necessarily mean that the government of the state has absolute authority. In free countries, the sovereignty belongs to the people, who may delegate only certain powers to the government, reserving other powers to themselves. In external relationships, sovereignty means that the state is completely independent of any authority outside itself.

STATE AND NATION. In the United States, we use the term *state* to mean one of the fifty component units of our federal union, and the term *nation* to mean the country as a whole. This is well enough so long as we are talking only about the United States, but these are not the real meanings of the words, and this usage can not always be applied to other countries. Properly speaking, a state is a community of people, inhabiting a more or less definite territory, possessing sovereignty, and living under a government with sovereign powers.

A nation is a community of people occupying a more or less definite territory, and having enough feeling of unity to consider themselves a distinct people. A common language may contribute to this feeling, but is not necessary to it. There are such bi-lingual or tri-lingual nations as the Canadians, the Belgians and the Swiss. If the people of a nation have a state of their own, and they always aspire to have one if they do not, we call it a national state. This condition is so prevalent today that we sometimes use the words state and nation interchangeably. Thus the world organization is called the United Nations, even though its members are sovereign states. The people of a nation may be divided among several states, as the Poles were formerly divided among Russia, Germany and Austria. Again, a state may contain several nations or parts of nations, as the old Empire of Austria-Hungary did and as the Soviet Union still does.

FEDERAL STATES. In terms of their exercise of sovereign powers, states may be either federal or unitary. A federal state, or federal union, has two (or possibly more than two) levels of government, each of which exercises sovereign powers; neither level can interfere with powers that belong to the other. Good examples are the United States and Canada. The constitution provides the basis for apportioning powers between the two levels. In the United States, the Tenth Amendment to the Constitution says, "The powers not delegated to the United States by the Constitution, nor prohibited by it to the states, are reserved to the states respectively, or to the people." In Canada it is done the other way; their constitution grants certain powers to the provinces, and all other powers are reserved to the Dominion.

UNITARY STATES. A unitary state is one in which only one level of government possesses sovereign power. Great Britain and France are good examples. There may be divisions of the country which have a large degree of self government, such as the British counties and municipalities, but they have only so much power as the central government permits them to have, and the national parliament can overrule anything they do. In unitary states we find varying degrees of centralization and decentralization. France is an example of a high degree of centralization. There is some local self government, but many matters which would be left to local units in the United States or Great Britain are administered by officials appointed by the government in Paris. At the other extreme, some unitary states are so decentralized that they narrowly miss being federal.

QUASI-FEDERAL STATES. There are a number of countries that are usually considered federal (they may even call themselves federal), but which could be better described as quasi-federal. Technically they are highly decentralized unitary states. They have the outward appearance of true federal unions, with component units that have their own constitutions and assigned powers. They differ from real federal states, though, in that the component units do not possess their powers in full sovereignty. Their national constitutions provide that, in certain contingencies, the national government may overrule the authority of the units. In a few of them (in South America) the national government may even suspend the unit governments and put the units under so-called "federal interventors." Countries of this type are the Federal Republic of Germany (West Germany), the Union of South Africa, and several countries in Latin America.

CONFEDERATIONS. We also hear of confederations. A confederation is an organization of sovereign states with machinery for meeting and planning joint action, but the final authority remains with the member states. There is no real government over them. This was the arrangement the United States had from 1781 to 1789 under the Articles of Confederation. It proved unworkable, so a real federal union under the Constitution was set up to replace it.

Kinds of Governments

MONARCHIES AND REPUBLICS. All people live under governments, but governments are of different kinds. In fact, no two sovereign states have governments that are just alike. However, some groups of governments do have enough characteristics in common so that they fall into definite classes. When the Constitution of the United States was being written, the classification that worried the founding fathers was monarchies and republics. They wrote into the Constitution every precaution they could think of to make sure that the country would never become a monarchy. Today, though, this classification means little. Except in some remote and backward countries, if monarchy survives at all, the monarch has become a mere ceremonial chief of state with no real discretion in matters of government. In such monarchies as Great Britain, Canada, Belgium, the Netherlands and the Scandinavian countries, the people govern themselves through elected representatives as truly as do the people of the United States. The late King Gustav V of Sweden once described his country as a "crowned republic," a term which well describes most present day monarchies.

RESPONSIBLE AND TOTALITARIAN GOVERNMENTS. The classification of governments that is most significant for our time is free or responsible governments and totalitarian governments. Free or responsible governments are often referred to as democracies, though this term can be applied only to their spirit and not to their form. Democracy as a *form* of government, meaning government directly by the people, can operate only on a very small scale, as in the old New England town meetings or the citizen assemblies in some of the smaller Swiss cantons. We consider a country democratic, though, when its government is effectively responsible to the will of a majority of the people.

Call them what we will, governments on this side of the

classification have certain distinctive characteristics. They are representative in that the governing power is in the hands of officials freely elected by the people. They are responsible in that policy making executive officials and the members of the law making body must answer for their actions in free elections in which the voters may turn these officials or their political party out of office and hand over the job of governing to another group or another party. Just as important, free governments are limited governments. There is a broad area of personal freedom of the individual with which the government has no power to interfere. In other words, the citizen has a number of civil rights which are not only guaranteed on paper, as in the English and American bills of rights and the French "Declaration of the Rights of Man," but are observed in practice and enforced by the courts. In some totalitarian countries such rights are promised in the written constitution, but are not respected by the persons in power in the government.

Major Types of Responsible Government

PRESIDENTIAL TYPE. Most free or responsible governments fall into one of two main types: the presidential type and the cabinet or parliamentary type. The government of the United States is the best example of the presidential type. In fact, it is our government that gave the name "presidential" to the type. We also find this type of government in most of the countries of Latin America, which copied it from us, and variations of it in a few countries in other parts of the world. It may be noted in passing that the mere fact that a government has an official called a president does not necessarily mean that such a country has the presidential type of government.

The most distinctive characteristic of this type of government is the principle of separation of powers. This means that the three branches of government are sufficiently independent that no one can be controlled completely by either or both of the others. There may be, as in the case of the American government, "checks and balances" by which each branch may restrict the other two. In contrast with the cabinet system, the

President and his cabinet can not be members of Congress and can take no direct part in its activities. In case of disagreement on policy, the President can not dissolve Congress and call an election for a new one; neither can Congress force the resignation of the President or his cabinet by a vote of censure or lack of confidence. The President is responsible for his acts, not to Congress, but directly to the people.

Another characteristic of the presidential type is that the highest official, usually but not necessarily called a president, is both chief of state and head of government. That is, he is both the ceremonial head of the country and the policy making executive. Under the cabinet system, these positions are held by different persons, as the King or Queen and the Prime Minister in Great Britain.

CABINET OR PARLIAMENTARY TYPE. The cabinet or parliamentary type of government developed in Great Britain during the eighteenth century and has been copied, with variations, by most of the countries of Europe and most of the newly emerging nations of Asia and Africa. Even as early as the Restoration Era (1660-1685) King Charles II found it necessary on two occasions to change his ministers (the executive officers through whom the royal power is exercised) to curry the favor of Parliament. The "Glorious Revolution" of 1688 deposed King James II and called William and Mary to the throne. It established the principle that the King holds his throne by the will of Parliament and therefore must govern in accordance with the wishes of Parliament. King William dutifully selected his ministers from the political party that had a majority in the House of Commons, and when there was a change in the party with a majority in the Commons, he changed his ministers. During his reign (1689-1702) and that of his successor, Queen Anne (1702-1714) it came to be accepted as a constitutional principle that the King (or Queen) acts only on the advice of the ministers, who assume the responsibility to Parliament for these royal acts, and so must resign if they lose the support of the House of Commons. However, the monarch still had his historic power to dissolve Parliament (actually, to dissolve the House of Commons) and call an election, but he could do this only on the advice of his ministers. Consequently, in case of a clash with Parliament, if the ministers believed that the voters would uphold their stand rather than that of Parliament, they could have the King dissolve Parliament and call an election.

The final step in the development of cabinet government came when, at the death of Queen Anne, the throne passed to her cousin George I, a middle aged German prince who could not speak a word of English and had no interest in British affairs. He stopped attending cabinet meetings. This vacuum in leadership was soon filled by developing the office of Prime Minister. Thus the Prime Minister became, and still is, the chief executive and the real head of government, while the King (or Queen) remains only as a ceremonial chief of state.

In typical cabinet government, the prime minister and all other ministers must be members of parliament; even in countries where they are not actually members, they can introduce bills and take part in parliamentary debate. Either way, they are at the same time the actual executive and a steering committee of parliament. Most important bills are introduced by cabinet members and no important bill can pass without cabinet approval. Thus cabinet government does not follow the principle of separation of powers, at least as between the executive and legislative branches. The courts, however, are kept independent to insure fair trials and even justice.

THE ROLE OF POLITICAL PARTIES. Political parties play an important role in most modern governments, even in totalitarian governments. They are especially important, though, in countries that have the cabinet type of responsible government. In countries that operate under a two party system, that is, having only two major parties, one in power and the other in opposition, the party that elects a majority of the members of the most directly elected branch or house of parliament is entitled to have its party leader appointed prime minister. The prime minister then selects the other cabinet ministers from members of his own party in parliament. If parliament fails to pass an important bill introduced by a cabinet minister, or if it passes a resolution of lack of confidence, the prime minister and cabinet may either resign or have parliament dissolved and an election called. If there has been no earlier occasion for a dissolution, parliament must be dissolved at the end of a certain length of time (five years in Britain) and an election called. Whenever an election results in the opposition party winning a majority of the memberships in the more directly elected house, the old prime minister and cabinet resign and the leader of the other party becomes prime minister.

However, only the English-speaking countries appear able to maintain a two party system very long. Elsewhere, if there is freedom of politics, people tend to divide into a large number of parties. We call this a multiple party system. With this condition, it is rare indeed for any one party to win a clear majority in parliament. This means that a cabinet can be formed only by a coalition of two or more parties, and this makes for instability and frequent cabinet crises. Whenever an issue arises on which the cabinet members of one of the parties in the coalition do not agree with the policy of the prime minister, that party's members in parliament will join with other parties already in opposition to pass a vote of lack of confidence, and the cabinet must resign. Then follows the ordeal of trying to put together a new coalition. The chief of state will ask one party leader after another to try to "form a government," until one finally succeeds in getting together a new coalition cabinet.

This situation is chronic in many countries of continental Europe. It was the inability to form a coalition in the German *Reichstag* in the early 1930's that made it possible for Hitler to come to power. More recently, it was the chronic instability of cabinets in France and their inability to agree on a policy for dealing with the rebellion in Algeria that caused the collapse of the Fourth Republic and the establishment of the Fifth Republic under General De Gaulle. Parliamentary dissolutions are rare in these multiple party countries, and often the constitution permits them only under most extraordinary circumstances. In most cases, a dissolution would not solve anything anyway, since an election would only shift the ratio of representation of the parties in parliament very slightly.

MIXED TYPE—FRANCE. The Fifth Republic in France, whose constitution was largely dictated by General De Gaulle, is an attempt to combine features of both the presidential and the cabinet types of government. The President is the effective head of government as well as ceremonial chief of state. Still, there is a Prime Minister as head of the cabinet, and the cabinet is still responsible to parliament, but with severe restrictions on the right of parliament to force the resignation of the cabinet by a no-confidence vote. A somewhat similar scheme is found in some of the newer countries, such as Egypt. The workability of this mixed arrangement appears to depend on the personality and political power of the president. There are grave misgivings as to how long it can survive the presidency of a towering figure like De Gaulle in France or Nasser in Egypt.

Totalitarian Government

WHAT IS TOTALITARIAN GOVERNMENT? There are two main elements in the concept of totalitarian government. First, it is total government. There is no area of human affairs over which the government does not exercise authority. Although a written constitution may say otherwise, the people have no rights which the government is bound to respect. Second, it is authoritarian. The ruling individual or group claims, on one pretext or another, to have an inherent right to rule; any challenging of this right is treason. There is no effective way in which such a government can be held responsible to the people. There may be a pretense of elections, but they are only a farce because the voters have no freedom of choice. The actual ruler may be changed by intrigue, assassination, *coup d'état* or civil war, but usually a totalitarian regime can be overturned only by violent revolution or defeat in a foreign war.

OLDER FORMS—ABSOLUTE MONARCHY AND MILITARY DICTATORSHIP. There are or have been many forms of totalitarianism. In one form or another, it is much older than free government. The oldest form of which we have historical record was absolute monarchy, which has now almost disappeared from the face of the earth. The monarch usually claimed divine authority. In the ancient Orient, he claimed to be a god or the descendant of a god. In early modern Europe, he claimed to rule by "divine right." God had selected him by the process of heredity and had endowed him with sovereignty, the right to rule. James I of England once declared, "Just as it is blasphemy to question what God can do, so is it treason to question what the King can do." Louis XIV of France is reputed to have said, "I am the state."

From time to time, in many parts of the world, there have been military dictatorships in which a military leader seized power by armed force, and held it until he was overthrown by armed force. There was no particular ideology involved other than the greed for power. In parts of Latin America, for several decades after the winning of independence, such dictatorship was so prevalent that it acquired a name. The individual dictator was called a *caudillo* (literally, leader) and the system was called *caudillismo* or caudillism. In monarchies, the man who seized power by force usually deposed the old king and became king himself. In republics, he usually called himself "president," and might make a pretense of following the constitution, but he always rigged the elections and imprisoned, killed, or drove into exile anyone who might challenge his authority. Sometimes, as in the case of the late General Rafael Trujillo of the Dominican Republic, the caudillo may put a puppet president in office to create an appearance of constitutional government, while retaining command of the military forces to insure the continuation of his dictatorial control.

IDEOLOGICAL TOTALITARIANISM. More important is the ideological totalitarianism which has made its appearance only in the present century. This usually takes the form of a party dictatorship, rather than a personal one, though it is often difficult to draw the line between them. Only one political party is permitted to operate. It nominates the only candidates for whom the people can vote and, through its leader, it dominates all the law making and policy making functions of the government. In Communist China and some of the Soviet satellites, a few minor parties are permitted so long as they do not stand for any independent ideas and co-operate with the dominant party in a permanent coalition. *The* party, which is always controlled from the top through appointed committees, claims virtual infallibility on the basis of a philosophy or ideology to which it adheres or claims to adhere.

FASCISTIC TYPE. The two principal versions of ideological totalitarianism are the fascistic and the communistic, which differ chiefly in the ideologies they claim to represent. The fascistic governments had their heyday in the decade of the 1930's, and most of them were destroyed or collapsed in World War II. First to appear was Fascism in Italy under Mussolini, which gave its name to the whole pattern. Next came Nazism in Germany under Hitler, and then Falangism in Spain under Franco. With the fall of France, in World War II, a fascistic type of regime was set up in the unoccupied portion of that country under Marshal Pétain. In the Western Hemisphere, Brazil and Argentina, for a time, had regimes that showed many of the features of Fascism.

Fascistic totalitarianism was characterized by extreme nationalism, holding that the glorification of the national state is the main function of government. In democratic theory, the state exists for the individual. As Jefferson put it in the Declaration of Independence, "To secure these rights, governments are instituted among men, deriving their just powers from the consent of the governed." In fascistic theory, on the contrary, the state is regarded as a vital organism, an end in itself. The relation of the citizen to the state is much like that of a cell in the body of an organism to the organism as a whole. The citizen, like the cell, exists for the benefit of the organism of which he is a part; thus the citizen has no individual rights of his own. He finds his "fulfillment" in the service of the state, in accordance with the directives of the party or the leader. In short, the citizen exists for the state, not the state for the citizen.

COMMUNISTIC TYPE. In communistic totalitarianism, the ideology is based on the doctrines of Karl Marx, who lived and wrote a full century ago. Marx maintained that the state, which ultimately should wither away, should exist for the workers. It should end the exploitation of the masses by the privileged classes. All classes but the workers should be "liquidated," thus producing a classless society. All industry and other means of production should belong to the workers jointly, and should be operated for their collective benefit. However, since Marx was extremely vague as to the structure of the state and its form of government, his doctrines had to be interpreted to apply them in revolutionary Russia. This interpreting was done by Nicolai Lenin, the first dictator of the Soviet Union, so the Russians talk of Marxism-Leninism. For a while, it was Marxism-Leninism-Stalinism, but Stalin has now been dropped from the trinity. In the Soviet Union, its satellites and Red China, the Communist Party is regarded as the guardian and interpreter of this infallible doctrine, and any deviation from it is treated as treason against the state.

There is another aspect of the Soviet type of totalitarianism, and that is its background in the autocracy of the Russian tsars. The old Russian Empire, in its turn, derived many of its features from the ancient Byzantine autocracy. In their authoritarian rule, their secret police, their censorship, their denial of civil rights, and their use of terrorism to suppress dissent, the Communists have continued ways of governing to which the Russians were accustomed under the tsars.

Later, we shall discuss some aspects of Soviet government. Details of some features of government differ in the satellite states, and even more in Communist China. The basic characteristics, though, are the same in all of them. In each there is a dictatorship of the Communist Party (which in some countries uses a different name) which controls every phase of life. In each case, this party claims the right to rule because it is the guardian and interpreter of Marxism-Leninism, which it declares to be the only basic truth.

Suggested Questions for Discussion

1. Anarchists claim that there is no need for government in the world. If you think they are wrong, why do you think so?
2. How and why must a government be both responsible and limited to qualify as a free or democratic government?
3. Why has the old distinction between republics and monarchies ceased to be significant?
4. Compare the advantages and disadvantages of federal and unitary states.
5. Communists often call their governments "democratic republics" or "people's republics." What do they mean?
6. How does the cabinet or parliamentary type of government conflict with the principle of separation of powers?
7. Which would you consider better: the presidential type of government or the cabinet type? Why do you think so?
8. Explain why old fashioned absolute monarchy was a form of totalitarianism.
9. What characteristics do all totalitarian governments have in common?
10. Contrast the philosophy of Fascism with the philosophy of democracy.
11. How do Communists justify totalitarian government?
12. Can you think of any conditions under which authoritarian government would be preferable to free or responsible government?

Bibliography

Barbu, Z., Democracy and Dictatorship (London, 1956)

Bowie, R. R., and Friedrich, C. J., Studies in Federalism (Boston, 1954)

Brown, D. F., Growth of Democratic Government (Washington, D. C., 1959)

Cole, T., European Political Systems (New York, 1959)

Cory, J. A., Democratic Government and Politics (Toronto, 1960)

Grimes, A. P., and Horwitz, R. H., Eds., Modern Political Ideologies (New York, 1959)

Kornhauser, W., Politics of Mass Society (New York, 1959)

Steinberg, S., Contemporary Governments in a Changing World (New York, 1959)

Verney, D. V., Analysis of Political Systems (New York, 1960)

Constitutions and Civil Rights

Sources and Types of Constitutions

WHAT IS A CONSTITUTION? We may define a constitution as the basis for a government. It sets up the framework of the government, the institutions through which the government operates, and the rules under which these institutions function. It is not necessarily a single document. It may include several documents and it may consist, in part or even entirely, of customs, traditions and usages. In this broad sense, we may say that every state or every country has a constitution. Even in the old absolute monarchies, and in the few that remain today in remote areas, there are institutions and long standing usages that provide the structure of government through which the monarch rules. In totalitarian states the constitution may be violated with impunity by those who rule, but these states always have a constitution, at least on paper.

SOURCES AND TYPES OF CONSTITUTIONS. Formerly, constitutions were classified into written and unwritten, with the American and British constitutions cited as the perfect examples. This classification, as we shall see, has become meaningless. We may better classify them according to their source into evolved, granted and drafted. The example *par excellence* of the evolved constitution is that of Great Britain. It has been built up over a period of nearly a thousand years. It includes a few documents, such as *Magna Carta* and the Bill of Rights, which are considered above ordinary law, but for the most part it consists of acts of Parliament and long established customs and usages. Legally, the power of Parliament is supreme. If Parliament passes an unconstitutional act, the effect is to change the constitution. Still, the pattern and rules of government are so firmly fixed in national tradition that the British constitution is one of the most stable in the world.

A granted constitution, usually in the form of a single document, is a charter given to the people of a country or one of its dependencies by the authority to whom those people owe allegiance. The charters of the thirteen American colonies, granted by the British crown and conferring a measure of self government, were early examples of granted constitutions. Similar charters have since been granted to other British colonies. During the nineteenth century, a number of European monarchs, usually under the threat of revolution, granted constitutions to their people which provided for elected parliaments and perhaps other measures of self government. Supposedly, the authority which granted the constitution could take it away, and in many instances this very thing occurred. It could happen, though, as it did in the case of the *Statuto fondamentale* granted to Sardinia-Piedmont by King Charles Albert in 1848 and which was later extended to the Kingdom of Italy, that the granted constitution would take such firm root that it became a higher authority than the king.

Most present day constitutions would be classified as drafted. Usually in the form of a single document, they were written by some person or group of persons who in form, if not always in fact, represented the people to be governed. In many cases, but not all, they were then approved or ratified by a vote of the people themselves. The first example of this type of constitution was *The Fundamental Orders of Connecticut* adopted in 1639 when the settlers, unable to obtain a charter because of disturbed conditions in England, drew up a frame of government for themselves as a makeshift until they could get a charter. The English tried the plan themselves in 1653 in Cromwell's *Instrument of Government,* but it did not work well and was soon abandoned. The real mother of drafted constitutions is the Constitution of the United States which went into effect in 1789. The French Revolution of 1789 started the writing of constitutions in Europe, and the scheme has now spread around the world.

CONSTITUTIONAL SYSTEMS. It is well to point out that the distinction between evolved and drafted constitutions is not always as clear as might seem. In any country that has lived under the same constitution for a long period of time, the actual working constitution will have changed drastically by evolution and interpretation, quite apart from changes made by formal amendment. If a foreigner, unfamiliar with the American government, should read the Constitution of the United States, he would get a very wrong impression of our institutions. He would have a badly distorted idea of how we choose our President. He would find no hint of a cabinet or of the power of our courts to pass on the constitutionality of laws. He would get a most inadequate picture of the powers of the President, Congress or the Supreme Court. The plain fact is that, while the written Constitution is the foundation of our constitutional system, much has been built on that foundation. Acts of Congress have set up our court system and spelled out the organization of the executive branch. Custom and usage have created the cabinet and the machinery by which we choose the president. In a thousand little things, not mentioned in the Constitution, we follow tradition.

If we compare our constitutional system, by which we mean the actual working arrangement of government, with what the British call their constitution, we find the same ingredients, with only a difference in emphasis. The first ingredient is fundamental documents that are above ordinary law. In our case, there is the Constitution of the United States with its amendments; in Britain's case, a number of documents, starting with *Magna Carta*. The second ingredient we may call "constituent statutes" (the British call them constitutional laws). These are acts of Congress or of Parliament which create or regulate organs of government. Third, we have customs, usages and traditions (in our case we sometimes call these our "unwritten constitution"). Finally, in both countries, the principles of common law have constitutional force.

Much the same would be true of the constitutional systems of other countries that have operated for a long time under the same constitution.

Varying Authority of Constitutions

CONSTITUTIONS AS SUPREME LAW. Anywhere there is an adopted constitution, it is, in theory, what the Constitution of the United States declares itself to be, "the supreme law of the land." If this is to be reality and not mere pretense, it must follow that any legislative or executive action which violates the constitution is null and void. If such constitutional supremacy is to be maintained, there must be some organ of government that can act independently of the executive and legislative branches, with authority to rule on the constitutionality of laws and executive acts. There can be no overruling its decisions on a point of constitutionality except by amending the constitution. Such is the situation in the United States.

In the United States, the function of sitting in judgment on the constitutionality of acts of Congress, or other organs of government, though not specifically granted in the Constitution, was assumed early in our history by the Supreme Court. Some countries, mainly in Latin America, where they have consciously copied our institutions, follow this same rule of "judicial review of legislation." In many instances, though, in these countries, the high court has been so "packed" by the president, that judicial review provides little protection either to the constitution or to the people against executive usurpation of power.

Some other countries have set up a special organ of government for this purpose, apart from the regular courts. Examples are the Constitutional Courts of Italy and the German Federal Republic (West Germany) and the Constitutional Council of the Fifth Republic in France. Only in Italy is this special court so constituted that it has complete independence of executive or legislative pressure.

Except in dictatorships, clear cut violations of the constitution are rare. Most questions of constitutionality hinge on the interpretation given to something in the constitution. Hence, the regular or special court that is charged with protecting the constitution against violation must also have the power to interpret the constitution, and its interpretation can be changed only by a later action of the same tribunal.

CONSTITUTIONS OF LESS AUTHORITY. The countries in which the constitution is actually safeguarded as supreme law are not very numerous. In totalitarian states and other dictatorships, the dictator or ruling group can violate the constitution at will because there is no effective way of holding him or them responsible. In parliamentary governments, the parliament, under the guidance of the ministers, is often considered the official interpreter of the constitution and hence the judge of its own powers. In this situation, ministers and members of parliament are restrained when tempted to play fast and loose with the constitution, first, by long standing customs and traditions; second, by political responsibility. The voter knows little and cares less about the fine points of constitutional interpretation. It may not disturb him at all if his parliament stretches the meaning of a constitutional provision to assume new powers, particularly if it uses the new powers in a manner that pleases him. But he is quick to resent any government action that tampers with his cherished institutions or infringes his rights. He can usually be depended upon to vote against any official or political party that so affronts him.

Elasticity of Constitutions

ELASTIC AND RIGID. Some writers classify constitutions into two groups, elastic and rigid. The difficulty with this classification is that there are varying degrees of elasticity and rigidity, and most constitutions fall somewhere between the extremes. The distinction is usually based on the ease or difficulty with which the constitution can be amended, but we must also take into account the ease or difficulty with which it can be changed in effect without formal amendment.

The only completely elastic constitution of any major country is that of Great Britain, where Parliament may change it by an ordinary act of legislation. In a sense, the constitution of the Soviet Union is also elastic. It may be changed at any time by a two-thirds vote of each house of the Supreme Soviet or national parliament. Since the Central Committee of the Communist Party, usually dominated by a single party leader, such as Stalin or Khrushchev, controls all the votes in the Supreme Soviet, that committee or its leaders can change the constitution at will merely by going through a bit of ceremony.*

CONSTITUTIONAL AMENDMENT. Most adopted constitutions make provision for amendment by a process somewhat more difficult and involved than ordinary legislation. The difficulty of the process determines the degree of elasticity. An amendment to the Constitution of the United States must first be passed by a two-thirds majority of each house of Congress and then ratified either by the legislature, or by a special convention elected for the purpose if Congress so directs, in each of three fourths of the states. In most of our states, an amendment is proposed either by a specified majority vote in the legislature (usually two thirds of each house) or by an initiative petition. It must then be ratified in a popular referendum.

In the Fifth French Republic, an amendment may be proposed either by the Premier and the President or by members of Parliament. It must then be passed in identical form by both chambers of Parliament and ratified in a popular referendum. However, the President may, instead of submitting the amendment to the voters, submit it to Parliament "convened in Congress," which means members of the two chambers meeting jointly as a single body. A three-fifths vote of this body is then required for ratification. This arrangement

---

* As this book goes to press, the Supreme Soviet has authorized Prime Minister Khrushchev to have a revision of the Soviet constitution prepared. When ready, it will undoubtedly be approved unanimously by the Supreme Soviet. It is unlikely that the revision will make very important changes in the structure of Soviet government, and it is certain that it will contain nothing that will weaken the control of the government by the Communist Party.

harks back to the constitution of the Third Republic which provided that members of the two chambers, meeting jointly at Versailles, instead of Paris, as a National Assembly, could amend the constitution by a simple majority vote.

The Italian constitution may be amended by Parliament alone provided both houses pass it by an absolute majority (a majority of the full membership, not just of those present when the vote is taken) on two occasions at least three months apart. However, unless each house gives the proposal a two-thirds majority on the second vote, a referendum may be forced by one fifth of the members of either house, a petition signed by 500,000 voters, or by five regional councils.

In West Germany, the constitution may be amended by a two-thirds absolute majority of both houses of Parliament. There is no provision for a referendum or other form of ratification. In East Germany, the *Volkskammer* (lower house of Parliament) may adopt a constitutional amendment provided a quorum of two thirds of the members are present, and two thirds of those present vote for the amendment. Here, likewise, no referendum is required. As in the Soviet Union, though, the Communist dictatorship makes this procedure a mere formality. Switzerland, being a federal union like the United States, follows both the federal principle and the democratic principle in its amending process. A constitutional amendment, proposed by the national legislature with a simple majority vote in each house, must be ratified both by a majority of the cantons and by a popular majority in a referendum. Obviously, we can not review the amending processes of all countries of the world, but most of those not mentioned follow some one or some combination of these patterns.

UNAMENDABLE PROVISIONS. Some constitutions state that certain provisions or features are not subject to amendment, at least by the ordinary process. The Constitution of the United States declares that "no state shall, without its consent, be deprived of its equal representation in the Senate." Presumably, this means that an amendment changing the basis of representation in the Senate would have to be ratified by all the states, not just the usual three fourths. The French constitution states, "The republican form of government shall not be subject to amendment," and the West German constitution declares that the basic principles of democratic federalism are unamendable. How far these prohibitions would hold up in a crisis is questionable. Certainly they could be changed by revolution or probably by overwhelming popular approval expressed in a plebiscite.

REVOLUTIONS. While we are on the subject, we should note that all constitutions are subject to change by revolution, and many have been so changed or even abolished. In this sense, a revolution is not necessarily an outbreak of violence. It may be defined as a change in the structure or personnel of government by illegal or unconstitutional means. The adoption of the Constitution of the United States, although it involved no violence, was a revolutionary act in that it violated the procedure for change set out in the Articles of Confederation. The French have a term, *coup d'état,* literally "stroke of state," by which they mean the seizure of power or a change in government structure by an individual or small group, in violation of the old constitution, but without a major outbreak of military violence. Needless to say, the French are not the only people whose constitutions have been changed in this way.

OTHER KINDS OF ELASTICITY. If we think of constitutional systems, rather than documents called constitutions, there may be elasticity that does not depend on the amending process at all. Legislative acts of the sort we have called "constituent statutes" may change or enlarge the structure of government. The new French constitution makes special provision for such acts, calling them "organic laws" and requires a different procedure for their enactment. Besides, the actual working of a constitution may be modified by the development of customs and traditions. The longer a constitution remains in effect, the more its practical operation will be changed by custom and tradition. The United States, Sweden and Switzerland are good examples of this kind of constitutional elasticity.

Desirable Qualities of Constitutions

DESIRABLE FEATURES. Political scientists have observed that there are certain features which make a constitution a more effective instrument of government, especially in a free society. Some measure of elasticity is essential to permit the adaptation of the constitution to changing conditions. Reasonable brevity is also an asset. The longer the document, the more detailed provisions it is likely to contain, and detailed provisions have a way of failing to meet the needs of changing times. The most detailed provision in the Constitution of the United States is that for electing the President and Vice President. Since the first two elections, it has never worked as intended, and it is now little more than a bit of red tape. Many of our American states have constitutions so long and detailed that they must be amended frequently and some have been completely rewritten several times. The constitution of the German republic set up after World War I was book length. Had it not been overthrown by Hitler, it almost surely would have broken down in a few years.

UNDESIRABLE FEATURES. From what has just been said, it is obvious that making amendment too difficult, and excessive length are objectionable features in a constitution. Another objectionable feature, closely related to excessive length, is the inclusion of what political scientists would call legislative material in the constitution. This refers to provisions which enact laws for the regulation of day to day affairs instead of merely empowering the legislative body to enact such laws. A case in point was the Eighteenth Amendment to the Constitution of the United States which prohibited the importation, manufacture or sale of intoxicating liquor. Had the principles of good constitution making been followed, the amendment would have granted Congress the power to prohibit. Had that been done, when the nation tired of the "noble experiment," only an act of Congress would have been needed to change it. As it was, we had to adopt the Twenty-first Amendment to repeal the Eighteenth. American state constitutions have been notorious offenders in this respect, but the national constitutions of many countries have fallen into the same fallacy.

Constitutional Guarantees of Civil Rights

PREVALENCE OF CONSTITUTIONAL GUARANTEES. Practically all constitutions contain, in some form, guarantees of the civil rights of citizens and, occasionally, of non-citizens. Even the British have their historic Petition of Right of 1628 and Bill of Rights of 1689, which are regarded as having constitutional force. Most of the early American state constitutions, adopted during the Revolutionary War, contained bills of rights following these British models. All but two of the thirteen French constitutions from 1789 to the present have either embodied the revolutionary "Declaration of the Rights of Man and of Citizen" of 1789 or have stated that it still has constitutional force. The original Constitution of the United States contained several guarantees of civil rights and, as a condition of ratification, a number of others were added in the first nine amendments. Practically all constitutions adopted since World War I contain similar guarantees. Even the constitution of the Soviet Union and the constitutions of the satellite states contain such guarantees.

VARYING EFFECTIVENESS. The effectiveness of these guarantees varies greatly from country to country. They are observed most faithfully in the English speaking countries because of a deeply ingrained tradition of personal freedom that goes back for centuries. Even in these countries, though, they are interpreted more narrowly and sometimes actually infringed in time of national crisis. At the other extreme are such totalitarian states as the Soviet Union. The personal rights listed in the Soviet constitution sound very impressive and liberal. In practice, though, they are either interpreted into meaninglessness or simply ignored by an irresponsible government. The totalitarian character of the Soviet government is not entirely to blame for this, however. Neither under the Tsars nor under the Soviets have the Russian people developed a tradition of personal freedom, and they do not miss what they have never had.

In other countries the effectiveness of civil rights guarantees falls somewhere between, depending largely on the national traditions in each country. France has a tradition of personal liberty that goes back to the great French Revolution of 1789. Except in times of major crisis, the liberties of Frenchmen are seldom infringed. Sweden has a tradition that goes back almost as far. In countries that have lived under responsible government for shorter periods of time, traditions of freedom are less firmly established and constitutional guarantees are less scrupulously observed.

SUSPENSION OF CONSTITUTIONAL GUARANTEES. Constitutions sometimes provide for the partial suspension of guarantees of civil rights in times of emergency. The Constitution of the United States says, "The privilege of the writ of *habeas corpus* shall not be suspended, unless when in cases of rebellion or invasion the public safety may require it." There is no mention of who shall have authority to suspend the privilege, but, since the statement occurs in the article on the legislative branch, it would appear that the power belongs to Congress. However, during the Civil War, President Lincoln suspended the writ in certain localities by executive order, and later persuaded Congress to ratify his acts.

The constitution of the Fifth French Republic directs the President, in case of certain emergencies such as a breakdown of the constitutional procedures, to "take the measures commanded by these circumstances" after consulting the Premier, the presidents of the assemblies and the Constitutional Council. President De Gaulle used this "emergency power" during one phase of the Algerian crisis to declare martial law. In constitutional monarchies it is usually a "prerogative of the Crown" to declare martial law, which suspends some of the constitutional guarantees, but he acts only on the advice of his ministers. Some Latin American constitutions permit the president, in specified emergencies, to suspend the constitutional guarantees. Others do what amounts to the same thing by permitting the president to proclaim a "state of siege."

From these examples, it follows that a formal suspension

of guarantees of civil rights is normally an executive act. However, legislative bodies sometimes pass laws that infringe the civil rights of some groups of persons, justifying such acts as necessary to national security. Where judicial review exists, either through the regular courts or through a special constitutional court, such acts of either the executive or the legislature may be upheld or invalidated by court action. A number of cases have reached the Supreme Court of the United States in which persons accused of being Communists or Communist sympathizers have claimed that the statutes under which they were convicted were unconstitutional because their civil rights were violated. In general, the Court has held that, if the actions of these persons constitute a threat to our national security, they may be deprived of some of their civil rights.

POLITICAL RIGHTS. By definition, civil rights are rights to personal freedom that are conferred on all citizens by the constitution or laws of the country. Political rights, that is the right to vote and to hold office, are sometimes confused with civil rights, but it is obvious that they do not fit the definition. These political rights, which really are privileges, are conferred by the laws of the country (or laws of the component units in a federal system such as the United States) only on classes of persons who are considered competent to exercise them in the interest of the general welfare. There are always restrictions as to age, residence and freedom from criminal record. Formerly, women were denied political rights everywhere, and in some countries they still are. At one time or another, many countries have had property or tax paying qualifications for voting, and some have had religious qualifications. Obviously, voting is not a civil right, and is not entitled to the same kind of protection.

HUMAN OR NATURAL RIGHTS. Also frequently confused with civil rights are those ideal freedoms which, in our time, are usually called human rights. In the days when our Declaration of Independence was written these were called natural rights on the theory that they are conferred, as Jefferson put it, by "the laws of nature and of nature's God." Whether we attribute them to "natural law" or to principles of humanity, they are freedoms which, many believe, every person should enjoy just because he is a human being, but they are only ideals with no standing in law. They are enforced only by common consent or by the pressure of public opinion. They become civil rights only when they are enacted into law.

Some years ago, a commission of the United Nations undertook to codify these in "The Universal Declaration of Human Rights." More than a hundred such "human rights" were listed in this document. The "Universal Declaration" merely set up ideals which it was hoped all countries would follow; it had no legally binding force. An effort was made also to draw up a "Covenant of Human Rights" which would have been submitted to member nations of the U.N. for ratification as a treaty, but the effort failed.

Constitutions and Limited Government

THE BASIS FOR LIMITED GOVERNMENT. Free government or limited government must, of necessity, rest upon a constitution, either evolved or adopted. Limiting the powers of government and making government responsible to the people are the primary functions of a constitution. How effectively a constitution performs these functions depends on the means of enforcement. In totalitarian states and other dictatorships, there is no real enforcement at all and the observance of constitutional provisions rests on the whim of the person or group in power.

JUDICIAL ENFORCEMENT. In the United States and in countries having special constitutional courts, provisions of the constitution are enforced by court action. This goes beyond judicial review of legislation. A wide variety of court procedures are available to enforce not only the guarantees of civil rights, but other provisions of the constitution.

EFFECT OF TRADITION. In countries where judicial remedies are not available, and to some extent in the countries where they are, officials are held to the observance of constitutional limitations on government mainly by the force of tradition. In nations like Britain, Sweden and Switzerland, which have long standing traditions, limited government is secure without other enforcement. In lands where such traditions are not well established, the course of government is apt to be disturbed by usurpation, *coup d'état,* or revolution. Even the device of holding government officials responsible politically depends for its effectiveness on the strength of tradition. That is why responsible government is apt to break down in new and inexperienced countries such as those that have gained their independence in recent years. Such traditions take time to build.

Suggested Questions for Discussion

1. What do you understand to be the real meaning of a constitution?
2. Could any government exist very long without some kind of constitution? Explain.
3. Why is the distinction between written and unwritten constitutions relatively unimportant?
4. Can a country have both a written and an unwritten constitution?
5. What are the important similarities and differences of the American and British constitutions?
6. How do you account for the wide variation in respect paid to national constitutions in different countries?
7. Should it be easy or difficult to change a national constitution? Why do you think so?
8. Practically all present day national constitutions contain guarantees of civil rights. What determines how effective these guarantees are?
9. Distinguish civil rights, human rights and political rights. Why would it be impossible to compile a complete and correct list of human rights?
10. Some constitutions permit the "suspension of constitutional guarantees." What are the arguments for and against such a provision?
11. Why is a constitution necessary to limited government?
12. What are some of the means used in different countries to assure the enforcement of constitutional provisions? Compare their effectiveness.

Bibliography

Bombwall, K. R., and Bhandari, D. R., Major Contemporary Constitutional Systems (Ambala, India, 1958)

Collins, I., Government and the Newspaper Press in France (New York, 1959)

Hayek, F. A., Constitution of Liberty (Chicago, 1960)

International Press Institute, Press Authoritarian Countries (New York, 1959)

Jennings, W., Ed., The British Constitution (Toronto, 1962)

Levy, L. W., Legacy of Suppression (Cambridge, Mass., 1960)

Meiklejohn, A., Political Freedom (New York, 1960)

Muller, H. J., Issues of Freedom (New York, 1960)

Spiro, H. J., Government by Constitution (New York, 1959)

Strong, C. F., Modern Political Constitutions (London, 1958)

THREE

Comparison of Legislative Machinery

Legislative Bodies

UNIVERSALITY. Back in the days of absolute monarchs, supreme legislative power belonged to the monarch. At his own pleasure, he could make a new law, or change or repeal an old one, just by issuing a decree. He might be advised by a council, whose members were either chosen by himself or determined by long tradition (or by a combination of the two), but such a council had only advisory power. In a few cases, most notably Great Britain, such a council evolved finally into a real legislature, but not until the eve of modern times.

Today practically every country has a legislative body whose members, in form if not in fact, represent the people. We shall discuss the different bases of representation in the following chapter. Known by different names in different countries, we use the word parliament as a general term to designate any of them. In totalitarian states the functions of the parliament may be only formal, but at least there is such a body and it meets from time to time. In personal dictatorships, the dictator may suspend the parliament, sometimes indefinitely, and rule by decree like the old absolute monarchs. Even in these cases, though, the parliament is rarely abolished and the expectation remains that, sooner or later, a new one will be elected.

BICAMERALISM. Most national legislatures are bicameral. That is, each consists of two divisions, or houses as we call them in English speaking countries. A few countries, such as Spain, Portugal and Greece, have unicameral (one house) parliaments. Members of the two houses are chosen in a different manner, and sometimes represent different constituencies. In English speaking countries we refer to the house that is least directly representative of the people as the upper house; elsewhere, it is usually called the second chamber. In some instances, the powers of the two houses are identical, but the tendency has been to reduce the powers of the upper house or second chamber. The United States is the only important country in which the upper house actually has more power than the more directly representative division, in its powers to approve treaties and confirm presidential appointments. In federal systems, the upper house may represent the component units (the states, in our case) while the other (sometimes called lower) house represents the people on the basis of population.

The "Mother of Parliaments"

EVOLUTION. It is fitting that we begin our discussion of national legislative bodies with the British Parliament, sometimes called "the mother of parliaments," because it has the longest unbroken history of any national legislature in existence. The actual history is that of the English Parliament, which became British only in 1707 when the Kingdoms of England and Scotland were united. Long before that date, though, the Scots had developed a national parliament modeled closely on the English.

The history of the English Parliament goes back more than a thousand years to the Witan of the Anglo-Saxons before the Norman conquest. The word Witan means wise men. It consisted of several hundred of the leading men of the realm, selected originally by the King, but holding membership for life and, in some cases, able to pass membership onto their oldest sons. They met at the call of the King and advised him on any questions he put before them. They had power to depose a King and, when the King died, they met without royal summons to elect a new King.

William the Conqueror, having first taken the pains to have himself elected King by the old Saxon Witan, changed the body into a feudal "Great Council," made up of his direct vassals. It lost the power to elect and depose kings, but several centuries later it regained that power. In the eyes of the King, the chief purpose of the Great Council was to provide him with money, but it did petition the King to issue laws, and sometimes withheld its grants of money until its petition was granted. In time, the feudal nobles who made up the Great Council were unable or unwilling to provide the King with all the money he needed, so the counties and selected towns were invited to send representatives to sit with the Great Council. The groups soon divided into the House of Lords and the House of Commons. Bit by bit, this "Parliament," so called because the members did so much talking, won the right to pass laws and control the finances, with the King retaining only a veto.

THE HOUSE OF LORDS. Parliament still consists of the House of Lords and the House of Commons. All hereditary peers are entitled to sit in the House of Lords and take part in its activities, but unless they are active in politics they rarely attend except for ceremonial occasions. There are twenty Lords Spiritual, the two archbishops and eighteen bishops of the Church of England selected on a rotating basis. They attend only when matters of concern to the Church are under consideration. There are nine "law lords," the Lords of Appeal in Ordinary, who are appointed for life and are the only members of the House of Lords who receive a salary. The House of Lords, along with being a part of Parliament, is the supreme court for certain classes of cases. When it is sitting as a court, only the law lords take part. They are trained lawyers and eminent jurists. They do not participate in legislative activity.

The King (or the Queen) may create new hereditary peers on the recommendation of the Prime Minister. Under a recent reform, the monarch may also appoint life peers, also on advice of the Prime Minister. It is the custom for elderly statesmen, retiring from active politics, to be offered a peerage, and they usually accept. These are about the only peers who take part in the regular activities of the House of Lords. Under this same reform, some women are also permitted to sit in the Lords. Thus, in effect, the House has become a body of elder statesmen whose accumulated knowledge and experience are of great value to the government and the nation.

Down into the eighteenth century, the House of Lords was more important and influential than the House of Commons. The balance has now shifted so that the House of Commons has supreme power in most legislative matters. In 1911, after a campaign to "mend or end the House of Lords," the Lords lost their equal power with the Commons except on private bills. If a money bill passes the Commons and is rejected by the Lords, it goes to the monarch for the royal assent (which, incidentally, is never refused) the same as if the Lords had passed it. The Lords may delay any other public bill for one year. If such a bill passes the Commons and is rejected by the Lords, it goes back to the Commons for reconsideration. If the Commons repass it in their next annual session, it does not go back to the Lords again, but is sent to the monarch for the royal assent. All money bills must originate in the Commons, and practically all other public bills do. The Lords can originate only private bills, and these are rarely of much importance.

THE HOUSE OF COMMONS. The House of Commons originated in the late 1200's as two "knights of the shire" from each county, and two citizens or burgesses from each of a number of towns selected by the King. They served without pay and at their own expense. Qualifications to vote for these members differed from place to place, but everywhere it was the privilege of a few men. After the sixteenth century, there was no change in the towns or "boroughs" represented until 1832. The industrial revolution of the 18th century brought the rise of many large communities that remained unrepresented, while a number of the older places shrank into "rotten boroughs" with only a few inhabitants, or "pocket boroughs" with no inhabitants at all so that the owner of the land could choose the two representatives.

Beginning with the "Great Reform Bill" of 1832, a series of reform measures, spaced through the next century, modernized the House of Commons completely. The entire country is divided into single member districts, called constituencies. Both men and women are eligible, and members are paid for their services. They are eligible for reelection indefinitely and are not required to live in the district they represent. They are elected for a maximum term of five years, but if Parliament is dissolved before that time, their terms end with the dissolution.

ORGANIZATION OF THE HOUSES. The organization of the two houses is very similar except that, as in the case of the American Senate, the House of Lords has its presiding officer provided for it. He is the Lord Chancellor, who is also the highest legal officer of the Kingdom with power to appoint most of the judges. He is a political officer and changes with party changes along with members of the cabinet. Like our House of Representatives, the House of Commons elects its own Speaker who must be one of its members. Although chosen initially as a party man, the British Speaker presides in a strictly non-partisan manner. It is the custom for each new House of Commons to reelect the former Speaker if he is still a member of the House, even if the party majority has changed. When a new Speaker must be chosen, the real choice is made by the Prime Minister, and the House elects the man he recommends.

As in our Congress, each House has its standing committees to which all bills are referred. There are fewer of them than in Congress and, except in dealing with private bills, they are of considerably less importance. The work on private bills is done mainly by the committees of the House of Lords. The physical arrangements in the British houses differ markedly from the usual pattern. In most legislative bodies the members sit facing the presiding officer, often in semi-circular rows of seats, and each member has a seat assigned permanently. The meeting chambers of both British Houses are long narrow rooms, with an open space running the length of the room. Flanking this space, are tiers of benches, something like church pews, where the members sit. Neither has enough seating to accommodate all of its members, but there are usually enough members absent so that this does not present a serious problem. Except for the "Lords Spiritual" section in the Lords, and the "government bench" and "opposition bench" in the Commons, no seats are assigned or reserved. At one end of the House of Commons, facing down the long aisle, is the Speaker's elevated seat with a table for clerks in front of it. In a corresponding position in the House of Lords is the throne, from which the "speech from the throne" is delivered, and, in front of it, a divan, called the "wool sack," on which the Lord Chancellor sits.

The American Congress

THE BASIS OF CONGRESS. The first national legislative body formed in imitation of the British Parliament was the American Congress. The Swiss Diet and the Dutch Estates General were older, but these were medieval bodies which had acquired some legislative powers. Both have long since been replaced with modern type parliaments.

The Constitutional Convention of 1787 adopted the bicameral plan for Congress, partly because it was traditional, but also to compromise the major conflict which the Convention faced. Delegates representing the smaller states wanted to keep the Congress of the Confederation: a one house group of delegations that represented the state governments, with each state having one vote. Delegates of the larger states, while favoring a two house Congress, wanted representatives in both houses to be chosen by the people and be apportioned according to population. The compromise was that the Senate should represent the state governments, each state having two Senators chosen by the state legislature. We still have two Senators from each state, but we no longer think of them as representing state governments as distinct from the people. The seventeenth amendment, adopted in 1913, provides for the direct popular election of Senators.

THE MAKE UP OF CONGRESS. Senators are elected for rotating six-year terms, one third being chosen at each biennial election. Members of the House of Representatives are chosen for two-year terms, and the entire membership is elected at each biennial election. Members of both houses are eligible for reelection indefinitely. Senators must be thirty years old; Representatives, twenty-five. Senators must have been citizens of the United States for nine years; Representatives, for seven. Both must live in the state from which they are chosen. Although the position of Senator carries more prestige, Senators and Representatives receive the same salary.

The Vice President of the United States is *ex officio* President of the Senate. Though a party man, he is expected to preside in an impartial manner. The Senate elects one of its own members President *pro tempore* (usually shortened to *pro tem*) to preside in the absence of the Vice President. The House of Representatives elects its own speaker. He is always a top leader of his party and presides as a partisan. Each house has a number of standing committees to which all bills are referred. Because of our separation of powers principle, these committees are much more important and powerful than their counterparts in European parliaments.

THE POWERS OF CONGRESS. Unlike the British Parliament, which is the judge of its own powers, being restrained only by tradition and political responsibility, the powers of Congress are strictly limited and are spelled out in the Constitution. Some powers, mostly bill of rights items, are forbidden both to Congress and to the legislatures of the states. Otherwise, all legislative powers not granted to Congress are reserved to the states. Congress shares its legislative power with the executive in a different manner than that of the British Parliament. In Britain, the royal veto atrophied from disuse a century and a half ago because the Cabinet, which would have to advise the use of the veto, is also the steering committee of Parliament and, as such, sponsors all important legislation. Under our separation of powers arrangement, the President can recommend legislation in his messages, but neither he nor members of his cabinet can participate directly in the work of Congress. The presidential veto, though, has remained very much alive. Congress can override the veto by a two-thirds vote of each house, but such a majority is usually difficult to obtain.

Like Parliament, Congress has the power of impeachment, but in neither country is it often used. In the United States, since the fiasco of the impeachment of President Andrew Johnson, it has become "unwritten constitution" that impeachment will not be used for political purposes. In Britain, where an adverse action by Parliament forces the resignation of the Cabinet, there is no occasion to resort to impeachment. Congress has constituent power in that it can submit amendments to the Constitution for ratification by the states. Parliament can amend the British constitution by a simple act of legislation.

In both countries the national legislative body has the final word on finance. In both, the executive prepares and submits the budget. In Britain, Parliament must accept or reject the budget entire, and a rejection calls for a resignation of the Cabinet. In the United States, Congress passes separate appropriation bills for various items in the budget, and may vote either more or less than the President has asked. Since a veto of appropriation bills is seldom feasible, the President must usually accept whatever Congress grants.

Continental Parliaments

VARIATIONS. In the "Free World" countries of continental Europe, the national parliaments vary considerably in structure. Most of them are bicameral, with the upper house or second chamber selected on a different basis from the lower or more popular. Here we can describe briefly only the more important of them.

THE FIFTH FRENCH REPUBLIC. The French Parliament consists of two chambers, the Senate and the National Assembly, though the constitution refers to the houses as "the assemblies." After unsatisfactory experiments with proportional representation under the Fourth Republic, members of the National Assembly are now elected by direct suffrage from single member districts. Parliament sets the terms of members by organic law, but as in the British House of Commons, their terms can be cut short by a dissolution of parliament. Under the Fourth Republic, the upper chamber, then called the Council of the Republic, was reduced to a mere advisory body like the British House of Lords. The present Senate, however, shares legislative power equally with the National Assembly and even has a few special powers of its own.

As compared with the Third and Fourth Republics, the powers of Parliament are restricted in several ways. Legislative acts which the Constitutional Council holds to be of a regulatory character may be modified by a presidential decree approved by the Council of Ministers (the Cabinet). Furthermore, the Cabinet (called the "Government" in the Fifth Republic) may ask Parliament to grant it power for a limited time to legislate by ordinance. These restrictions, coupled with the near impossibility of Parliament's forcing a resignation of the Cabinet, definitely subordinate Parliament to the President as a policy making organ of government.

Members of the Cabinet may not be members of either house of Parliament, but they have access to either house at all times. Thus, while they can not vote or serve on committees, they can take part in parliamentary debate, a privilege denied to Cabinet members in the United States. Either a member or the Prime Minister may introduce bills, but as in Britain, bills sponsored by the Cabinet have top priority. Private members' bills which would either reduce the revenue or increase expenditures can not be considered. The President of the Republic may, after consultation with the Prime Minister and the presidents of the two chambers, dissolve the National Assembly, but he can not order another dissolution within a year.

Parliament can force the resignation of the Cabinet only in two circumstances, and in both the initiative must come from the Prime Minister. The Prime Minister may "pledge the responsibility of the Government" on general policy, which means that he may ask for a vote of confidence. To take up the challenge, the Assembly must pass a vote of censure, sponsored by one tenth of the members, and voted, after a forty-eight-hour delay, by an absolute majority of all the members. Only if this vote of censure is passed is the Cabinet required to resign. The other possibility is that the Prime Minister may "pledge responsibility" on a particular bill. In this case, the bill is considered passed unless a vote of censure, proposed within twenty-four hours, is adopted by the Assembly. The Prime Minister may also ask the Senate for approval of a policy, but the only effect of this is the influence it might have on the Assembly.

Unlike the arrangement in most countries, the two chambers of the French parliament meet in different buildings, some distance apart. In each, the seats are arranged in concentric semicircles facing the presiding officer's chair, with members belonging to different political parties ranged from the presiding officers' right to his left in the order of their conservatism or radicalism. The French have used this seating arrangement ever since the time of the Revolution of 1789, and it has given rise to the terms "right" and "left" to denote conservatism and radicalism respectively. Procedural rules are similar to those of most other parliamentary bodies.

There is also an Economic and Social Council, the composition of which is determined by organic law. At present, its members are appointed by the President of the Republic. Its functions are strictly advisory. Either the Cabinet or Parliament may call upon it for advice. Its chief role at present is to strengthen the President as a policy maker.

THE REPUBLIC OF ITALY. The Parliament of Italy under the republic, established at the close of World War II, resembles the Parliaments of the Third and Fourth Republics in France. It is bicameral, with the two chambers having equal powers. Unlike most cabinet governed countries, where cabinet responsibility is only to the lower house, both houses of the Italian Parliament must concur in a vote of confidence or a vote of censure.

The lower house, called the Chamber of Deputies, as it was under earlier French constitutions, consists of one deputy for each 80,000 persons, elected by direct suffrage for a maximum term of five years. Deputies must be twenty-five years old, the same as Representatives in the United States Congress.

The upper house is called the Senate. Senators, who must be forty years old, are elected in groups from regions, with one Senator for each 200,000 population in the region. Most regions have six or more. Voters in the election of Senators must be twenty-five years old. The President of the Republic may appoint, as Senators for life, five persons who are eminent in cultural fields. All ex-Presidents of the Republic are Senators for life. Elected Senators serve for six-year terms unless Parliament is dissolved sooner.

Bills may be introduced by the Cabinet, by any number of either chamber, or by initiative petition. Since Cabinet members are also members of Parliament, government bills usually have priority, but not to the almost complete exclusion of private members' bills that we find in Britain and France. Powers of the executive branch to issue "decree laws" are strictly limited. After passage by Parliament, any bill except a financial measure must be submitted to a popular referendum if demanded by petitions signed by a prescribed number of voters.

The power of the Parliament to force the resignation of the Cabinet is more restricted than in most cabinet governed countries, but less than in the Fifth French Republic. Failure to pass a Cabinet-sponsored bill does not force a resignation. This can be done only by failure to pass a vote of confidence when the Prime Minister has asked for it, or by the adoption of a vote of censure by both houses. A newly appointed Cabinet must ask for a vote of confidence within ten days after its appointment. After that, the asking for such a vote is at the discretion of the Prime Minister. As in France, a vote of censure must be introduced by a petition signed by one tenth of the entire membership, but this must be ten percent of the entire membership of both houses, whereas in France it is only ten percent of the Assembly. Unlike most countries with a similar scheme of government, a dissolution of Parliament applies to both Houses. In most countries, it is only the lower house that is dissolved. Seating arrangements and procedural rules are similar to those of the French Parliament. There are standing committees which consider bills, but they are far less important than similar committees in the American Congress.

WEST GERMANY. The Federal Republic of Germany (the official name for West Germany) has a bicameral parliament called the Diet. This name comes from the Latin word *dies* meaning day. The Germans have always used the word *Tag*, German word for day, to mean an assembly. Thus, in the old Holy Roman Empire, the assembly of princes was called the *Reichstag*, Diet of the Empire. The name *Reichstag* was retained under the German Empire (1871-1918) and the Weimar Republic to mean the popularly elected house of the Diet.

The present Diet consists of the *Bundesrat* (Council of the Union) and the *Bundestag* (Assembly of the Union). In line with the federal principle, the *Bundesrat* represents the *Länder* (lands) or, as we should call them, the states. Each *Land* (state) has at least three members; it has four if its population is between 2,000,000 and 6,000,000; five if its population exceeds 6,000,000. These *Bundesrat* members are also members of the cabinets of their respective states and must vote under what, in our party conventions, we call the "unit rule"; the delegation from each state casts three, four or five votes as a bloc for or against a motion.

The *Bundestag* is the popularly elected house. The constitution provides that its members, who must be twenty-five years old, shall be elected for four-year terms (unless ended by an earlier dissolution) by universal suffrage and secret ballot. The number and distribution of memberships is left to ordinary law. A law of 1953 sets the number at 484, and provides that half of these be chosen in single-member districts of approximately equal population. The other half, apportioned among the states according to population, are elected from party lists in each state under a plan of proportional representation of parties. A party getting less than five percent of the vote in a state receives no representatives at all.

Bills are introduced into the *Bundestag* by the Chancellor or a member. When passed by the *Bundestag* a bill goes to the *Bundesrat* for action. If rejected by this second chamber, the bill goes back to the *Bundestag* for reconsideration. If repassed there by the same proportion of votes by which the *Bundesrat* rejected it, it becomes law anyway. Cabinet ministers are responsible directly only to the Chancellor, but if a Chancellor were forced to resign, his Cabinet would go out with him.

In theory, the Chancellor is responsible to the *Bundestag*, but in some cases he may override its authority and the procedure for forcing his resignation is such as to make this all but impossible. If the Diet fails to pass his budget, he may direct expenditures necessary to carry on the government. He may strike out appropriations that exceed his budget items. If the *Bundestag* refuses to pass an important bill the Chancellor wants, he may declare a "legislative emergency," in which case the bill becomes law if passed by the *Bundesrat* alone. He may have the President dissolve the *Bundestag* in case of a deadlock. The *Bundestag* may force the resignation of the Chancellor by a no-confidence vote, but two days must elapse between the introduction of the no-confidence resolution and the vote on it, and it must pass by an absolute majority of all members. To make it even more difficult, the resolution must name the new Chancellor, a point on which it would be extremely difficult to get agreement among opponents of an administration.

As in most legislative bodies, each chamber of the Diet elects its own presiding officer and adopts its own rules of procedure, which rules are very similar to those found in other parliaments. There are standing committees, but they usually just follow the recommendations of the Chancellor.

OTHER CONTINENTAL COUNTRIES. We can mention only a few peculiarities of the other Free World countries of continental Europe. The parliaments of the Netherlands and Belgium follow the British pattern, with some variation, with their equivalents of Lords and Commons. Switzerland being a federal union, its parliament resembles that of other federal states. The upper chamber, called the Council of States, represents the cantons even more than our Senate represents the states. Each canton has two members, but they are chosen for such terms and in such manner as the individual canton decides;

some are elected by popular vote, while some are chosen by the canton legislature. Their terms vary from one year to four years. The lower house, called the National Council, consists of two hundred members apportioned among the cantons according to population and elected for four-year terms under proportional representation. The two chambers have identical powers though, in practice, the Council of States usually approves all bills passed by the National Council. There is no ministerial responsibility and no provision for dissolution.

The Scandinavian countries are all constitutional monarchies operating with a cabinet system and bicameral parliaments. In Sweden, both chambers are elected under proportional representation. The upper chamber of 150 members is chosen by the county councils for eight-year terms. The 230 members of the lower chamber are elected for four-year terms by direct suffrage, from twenty-eight districts. All committees are joint committees of the two houses. The ministers are legally responsible to the lower chamber, but cabinet crises are rare. Dissolutions of parliament are possible, but rarely occur. The Danish parliament resembles the Swedish in most respects with the notable difference that nineteen of the seventy-six members of the upper chamber are appointed. The King may dissolve the lower chamber at any time, but may dissolve the upper only under special circumstances. The Norwegian Parliament is peculiar in that its 150 members are elected without indication in which chamber they will serve. They then divide themselves into the two chambers, one third of the members in the upper and two thirds in the lower.

OTHER FREE WORLD COUNTRIES. Most of the Latin American nations have copied the structure of the United States Congress. The nations of the British Commonwealth all have the cabinet system so that their parliaments function much as does the British Parliament. In structure, however, they have drawn on both British and American patterns. In Canada, the House of Commons is very like its British prototype. Their upper house, called the Senate, consists of members appointed for life. The Australian Parliament follows rather closely the model of our Congress. The House of Representatives, like its

American namesake, consists of members apportioned among the states according to population and elected from single member districts. There are six Senators from each of the six states regardless of population. A peculiarity of the Japanese House of Representatives is that its members, elected for four-year terms by universal suffrage, are chosen from multi-member districts in which the voter votes for one candidate only. This provides a sort of proportional representation. Members of the Japanese upper house, called the House of Councillors, are chosen by the same electorate, but one hundred are elected at large and 150 from the prefectures. Its powers are restricted in a manner similar to those of the British House of Lords. Most of the new nations of Asia and Africa have modeled their parliaments on those of the countries of which they were formerly dependencies.

Parliaments in Totalitarian States

PARLIAMENTS IN NAME ONLY. Most totalitarian states, Communist or otherwise, have some kind of body which is a parliament in name and, in form, may have extensive legislative and financial powers. Without exception, though, this is only a group of "yes men," hand picked by the dictator or party oligarchy, with the voters having no freedom of choice. The only real functions of such a "parliament" are to provide an audience for speeches by the dictator or party dignitaries and to approve unanimously what the ruler or the party has decreed. In military dictatorships there is usually provision for a parliament, but it either is never elected or is not permitted to meet.

THE SOVIET UNION. The Supreme Soviet of the Soviet Union fits this general description, but a bit needs to be said about its structure. It consists of two soviets or councils, of more than a thousand members each. The Soviet of the Union represents the governmental divisions of the country: the union republics and the autonomous republics. The Soviet of Nationalities represents the various national and language groups. They meet twice a year, but usually for less than a week in each session. For legislative routine, in which they only approve by acclamation measures put before them by the ministry or the presidium, they meet as two chambers. For other business, such as amending the constitution, electing the presidium, electing the ministers, and ratifying the appointment of diplomats, military officers, and a few other officials, they meet as a single body. They meet in a large rectangular hall with all seats facing the front of the room, more like an audience than like a deliberative body. The only debate that ever takes place is prearranged for propaganda effect.

THE PRESIDIUM. A distinctive feature of the Soviet structure is the presidium. This is a continuing joint committee of the two branches of the Supreme Soviet, with about a hundred and fifty members, drawn from both chambers and from all parts of the country. When the Supreme Soviet is not in session, the presidium performs all the routine functions of a parliament. About the only things it can not do on behalf of the Supreme Soviet are amend the constitution and vote the budget. The president of the presidium, while he is not a chief of state in the usual sense, does perform the functions of a chief of state which can not be dispensed with, such as receiving diplomats and writing courtesy notes to other chiefs of state.

The Legislative Process

PROCEDURE. In most national legislative bodies, bills may be introduced by any member of either chamber. In a few, such as Norway, all bills must originate in the lower house. A larger number of countries follow the same rule as the American Congress that all bills for raising revenue or appropriating money must originate in the lower chamber. In Switzerland, every bill is introduced simultaneously in both chambers to avoid delay.

After consideration by committees, bills are debated on the floor of the house (usually, each house in turn), at which time amendments may be offered and voted upon. In the British House of Commons, government bills are never amended in this way because the adoption of an amendment would call for a resignation of the Cabinet or a dissolution of the House. At the debate stage, both houses of the British Parliament and the American House of Representatives (as well as the lower chambers in a few other countries that have copied the idea), use the device of Committee of the Whole House. This is legal fiction by which the house acts as a committee, rather than in its capacity of a law making body, in order to have less stringent rules of debate, to be able to take test votes that are not binding, or to get more effective discussion, particularly of financial measures.

After the debate, bills are voted on for passage. Usually, a majority vote of members present, if a quorum is present, is sufficient for passage. Some measures designated by the constitution require a special majority, such as two thirds or an absolute majority (a majority of all members elected, not just a majority of those present). Methods of voting vary widely with different parliaments or even in the same body. Ordinarily, unless the rules are suspended in an emergency, voting by acclamation is permitted only on procedural matters. In the British House of Commons, the vote on final passage is taken by "division of the house." Members go from the chamber to "division lobbies" on either side of the main hall, those who favor the bill on one side, those who oppose it on the other. Then they reenter their meeting room in single file through narrow doors and are counted by clerks as they enter. Both houses of the American Congress use the same method, except that they do not leave their chamber. First those who favor the bill, then those who oppose it, file past the clerk's desk to be counted. For important measures, our Congress takes a "vote of record." The clerk calls the roll and each member, as his name is called, stands and votes "yea," "nay" or "present." If he votes "present," he is counted toward a quorum, but is recorded as abstaining on the vote. The French National Assembly uses four methods of voting: a show of hands, a standing vote, a vote by ballot (using different colored slips of paper for yes, no and abstaining) and a vote of record. The ballot vote is not strictly secret, since other members can see the color of the slip a particular member is putting in the basket as the clerk collects them, but it is not recorded. In the French vote of record, each member takes his colored slip to the clerk's desk and a record is kept of how he voted. In contrast to the free countries, voting in the Russian Supreme Soviet is always by acclamation and is always considered unanimous.

EXECUTIVE LEADERSHIP. In practically all countries there is a tendency to look to the executive for legislative leadership. In totalitarian states, this goes to the length of complete executive domination, the parliament merely approving by acclamation whatever the executive directs. In countries like the United States which follow the separation of powers principle, the executive (in our case, the President) can only recommend legislation in his messages. The President can, if he chooses, deliver his message orally as an address to a joint session of the two houses but, beyond that, he can take no direct part in the work of Congress. He may exert influence in conferences with committee chairmen and in other indirect ways, but he can not steer a bill through Congress. His cabinet members have no contact with Congress except when they are called as witnesses in committee hearings.

In most cabinet governed countries, the prime minister and his cabinet are usually members of one house or the other and so can take full part in debate and in managing bills on the floor. This makes executive leadership fully effective. Even in countries like West Germany and the Fifth French Republic, where the ministers are not members of parliament, they may address either house at any time. Moreover, the French President and the West German Chancellor hold a club over their parliaments that the American President does not have, in that they can dissolve the lower house and compel the members to seek reelection at almost any time.

CABINET VERSUS COMMITTEES. Practically all legislative bodies have committees to which bills are referred for consideration and screening and to which some other duties are sometimes assigned. Committee arrangements and the importance of their work differ widely in different countries. In the American Congress, the standing committees do practically all the work of preparing and screening legislation. In cabinet governed countries, though, the cabinet does the bulk of this work on all measures that are considered public bills. This is particularly true in the British House of Commons where the four standing committees on public bills do little more than scrutinize the proposals of the Cabinet. In the French National Assembly, the committees act almost as independently as those in the American Congress, though they usually maintain closer contact with members of the ministry. A distinctive feature of the French committees is that their reports are not made by their chairman, but by a member who is selected as "reporter" for a particular bill. This member then steers the bill through the debate and the vote. In the House of Commons, this is always done by a cabinet minister. In Congress, it is done by the chairman of the committee. Most other countries follow either the British or American usage.

Each of the two arrangements, domination of the legislative process by committees and domination by the cabinet, has its good points and its bad ones. For the committee plan it may be said that it maintains the separation of powers principle, in which Americans generally believe, and preserves the independence of the legislative body. Through committee hearings, divergent interests may be presented, and legislation as worked out by the committees is more likely to represent a compromise of interests than are measures decided upon in closed meetings of a cabinet. It has the disadvantage that, while we hold the President responsible politically for a legislative program, we do not give him adequate means to get his program enacted. The cabinet arrangement avoids the deadlocks that so often occur between our President and Congress, but it tends to reduce the legislative body to little more than a check on the executive.

Financial Control

NATIONAL FINANCE. In theory, every national legislature has final control of government finance, with power to levy taxes, borrow money, and appropriate money. As national finances have become more complicated, nearly all countries have adopted some form of executive budget, but the importance of this budget varies greatly from country to country.

PARLIAMENTARY CONTROL. In the United States, the Scandinavian countries and a few others, the executive budget is a carefully worked out estimate of the needs of all departments and agencies, but it is presented to the legislature only as recommendations for appropriations. The executive may also make recommendations for taxes or loans. But, having received these recommendations, the legislature takes matters into its own hands. It originates its own bills for taxes, loans and appropriations. It may follow or ignore the executive recommendations, and rarely gives the President or the Finance Minister all he has asked for. In these countries, parliamentary control is complete and final.

PARLIAMENTARY VETO. In Great Britain, Switzerland, and most countries having the cabinet system, the parliament has only what amounts to a veto on the executive budget. In these countries, the budget, which includes taxes and bond issues as well as expenditures, is prepared by the minister of finance (called "Chancellor of the Exchequer" in Britain and "the Chancellor" in Switzerland) with the approval of his cabinet colleagues. This officer then presents the budget in parliament and defends it in the parliamentary debate. In Switzerland, the parliament can modify the budget, but rarely does. If it should, the executive (the Federal Council), like the American President, must just make the best of it. In Britain and other cabinet governed countries, the parliament must accept or reject the budget entire, and a rejection calls for either the resignation of the cabinet or a dissolution of parliament.

EXECUTIVE CONTROL. In France and West Germany, the budget (which also includes taxes and loans) is prepared under the direction of the head of government (the President in France, the Chancellor in West Germany) and is submitted to Parliament for action. In France, if the National Assembly fails to approve the budget within forty days, the cabinet may refer it to the Senate. If the Senate approves it within fifteen days, it is considered enacted. If neither chamber has approved it within seventy days, it may be put into effect by ordinance or executive order. In West Germany, if the *Bundstag* fails to vote the budget, the Chancellor may authorize any expenditures he considers necessary for carrying on the government, and he can, in certain emergencies, authorize expenditures in excess of the budget appropriations. In totalitarian states, parliamentary approval of the budget is a mere formality.

Suggested Questions for Discussion

1. Is there any valid reason for calling the British Parliament "the mother of parliaments"? If so, what is it?
2. Point out the important similarities of and differences between the British Parliament and the American Congress.
3. Of what use, if any, is the House of Lords?
4. Compare the effective powers of parliament in: (1) Great Britain, (2) France and (3) West Germany.
5. In what significant ways is the legislative process different in the United States and in cabinet governed countries?
6. Compare the structure of parliament in: (1) France, (2) West Germany and (3) Italy.
7. Point out some distinctive peculiarity of the parliament of each of these countries: (1) Italy; (2) West Germany; (3) Sweden; (4) Norway; (5) Japan.
8. What countries, if any, have unicameral parliaments? What federal unions have unicameral legislatures in their component units?
9. What is a usual characteristic of the "upper house" or "second chamber" in federal unions?
10. Compare the ways in which financial control is exercised by: (1) the American Congress, (2) the British Parliament, (3) the West German parliament and (4) the Swiss parliament.
11. Why do totalitarian states have parliaments? How do these parliaments operate?
12. Describe the Supreme Soviet of the Soviet Union. What is the presidium?

Bibliography

Campion, Lord, and Lidderdale, D. W. S., European Parliamentary Procedure (London, 1955)

Dunnico, Sir Herbert, Mother of Parliaments (New York, 1951)

Hansard Society, Parliamentary Reform, 1933-1958 (London, 1959)

Jennings, Sir Ivor, Parliament (Cambridge University, 1948)

Kersell, J. E., Parliamentary Supervision of Delegated Legislation (London, 1959)

King-Hall, S., and Ullmann, R. K., German Parliaments (New York, 1954)

Raalte, E. van, Parliament of the Kingdom of the Netherlands (London, 1959)

Young, R. A., The British Parliament (London, 1959)

FOUR

Representing the People

Bases of Representation

REPRESENTATIVE AND NON-REPRESENTATIVE GOVERN-
MENTS. Almost all present day governments claim to be based
on popular sovereignty and to represent the people. There are
still a few comparatively unimportant countries in remote areas
of the world that work on the theory that all power comes
from the monarch, but these need not detain us. In totalitarian
countries the representation of the people is little more than a
pretense, but in the Free World popular representation is a
reality. Executives are usually elected, at least indirectly, and
so may be regarded as representing the people of the nation
as a whole. However, it is to the legislative bodies that we
look for direct representation.

HOW DO LEGISLATIVE BODIES REPRESENT THE PEOPLE?
Almost everywhere, members of what we should call the lower
house are elected directly by the voters. Members of the upper
house or second chamber are sometimes elected indirectly and,
in federal states, they usually represent the component units.
In the United States, until the election of 1914, after the
Seventeenth Amendment had gone into effect, Senators were
not only apportioned equally among the states but were chosen
by the state legislatures. In West Germany, members of the
Bundesrat are apportioned among the *Länder* or states roughly
according to populaton, but they are members of the state
cabinet, selected in each *Land* by their cabinet colleagues. In
Switzerland, members of the Federal Council or Council of
States are, like our Senators, apportioned two to a canton, but

they are chosen in any manner and for any term the canton itself may provide. In the Fifth French Republic, a unitary state, Senators are elected indirectly by electoral colleges. In Italy, Senators are elected directly from single member districts combined with regional party lists, but voters must be twenty-five years old to vote for them. In a few countries, such as Britain, members of the upper house are partly hereditary, partly appointive. In Canada, the Senators are appointed. In Japan, members of the House of Councillors are chosen by the same voters who choose members of the House of Representatives, but one hundred of the 250 members are elected at large and 150 from the prefectures.

REPRESENTATIVE DISTRICTS. Members of the lower house are usually apportioned according to population and are elected from local districts. If the country is federal, these districts are subdivisions of the component units and are usually marked out by some agency in the unit itself. Thus, in the United States, "congressional districts" are marked out by the state legislatures. In unitary states, the districts are marked out originally by national law, though some other arrangement may be provided for redistricting to meet changes in population. In Great Britain, this is done, not at stated times but as population shifts occur, by local commissions.

SINGLE MEMBER DISTRICTS. In the United States, Great Britain, the Fifth French Republic, Canada, and a number of other countries, members of the lower house are chosen from single member districts. In countries where there are only two major parties, each party nominates a candidate and the one who receives the largest popular vote is elected. In Britain, party names do not appear on the ballot. Anyone who can get ten signatures to a nominating petition and who puts up a deposit of £150 gets his name on the ballot as a candidate. If the candidate receives more than one eighth of the popular vote, his deposit is refunded. Despite this superficial appearance of non-partisan election, no candidate has a chance who is not "adopted" by a party organization, and the voter is more apt to be voting for the party than for the individual candidate.

In France, which has a multiplicity of parties and has long

been accustomed to multiple member districts with proportional representation, the present electoral law is an innovation which may not last long. Each party nominates a candidate in each district. In the first balloting, if any candidate receives a clear majority of all votes, he is elected. If no one receives such a majority, a second balloting is held a week later in which the candidate who receives a plurality is elected. In West Germany, the present electoral law (which may be changed by ordinary legislation) provides that 50% of the *Bundestag* members shall be chosen from single member districts. The others are chosen by proportional representation.

MULTIPLE MEMBER DISTRICTS. In many countries, members of the lower house are chosen in multiple member districts, usually under some plan of proportional representation for political parties. It would be possible, of course, to have multiple member districts without proportional representation, but this is not done in any important country except in the selection of state delegations in the upper house in federal unions. Multiple member districts are found normally in multiple party countries, along with proportional representation, in order to provide representation for the many parties. In some countries, very small parties are denied representation. In West Germany, for example, a party that receives less than 5% of the total vote receives no representation. This is intended to discourage the indefinite splintering of parties.

PROPORTIONAL REPRESENTATION. The idea of proportional representation is to give each political party representation in the legislative body approximately in proportion to its strength among the voters. Obviously there is little need for such a device in a country that has only two major parties, so that one or the other almost always wins a clear victory in an election. There are several schemes of proportional representation, but all involve the choice of representatives from multiple member districts. Probably the simplest is that used in electing members of the Japanese House of Representatives. They are chosen in small multiple member districts, with each voter voting for only one candidate. The total result may not be a very close approximation of the voting strength of the parties, but at least all parties are assured of some representation. Most of the plans are more complicated and are based on voting for party lists. By various mathematical formulas, an effort is made to award memberships from the various party lists in proportion to the votes cast for the various parties. Usually the order in which names are to be selected from the list is determined by the party organization that makes up the list. In Italy, however, the voter may indicate the order of his preferences on the party list and memberships are awarded by averaging up these preferences. Sometimes groups of parties are permitted to present coalition lists (they were in the Fourth French Republic) which gives the group an advantage over individual parties with separate lists. Occasionally, such a group will succeed in passing a "rigged" electoral law which gives any list receiving a certain percentage of the vote, well short of a majority, a majority of the memberships in the legislative body. In most systems, the number of memberships awarded in a district from a party list is determined by dividing the votes for that party by a previously determined "electoral quotient," so that there are always remainders of less than a quotient. In some countries, Italy for example, these remainders are applied to the election of party members from national lists.

TOTALITARIAN STATES. In totalitarian states, the legislative body is so completely controlled by the party oligarchy that it makes little difference what formula is followed in electing the members. In the Soviet Union, members of both houses of the Supreme Soviet are sent from single member districts, but in each district there is only one candidate. In East Germany, members of the *Volkskammer* or lower house are chosen under proportional representation. This is meaningless, however, because only parties that follow the Communist line are permitted to participate. Members of the *Länderkammer* or upper house are elected by the legislatures of the *Länder* or states to keep up the appearance of federalism. Other satellite states have different formulas, but they all add up to the same thing: members of the legislative body are hand picked by the Communist party oligarchy. Hence, they represent the people only in a distorted sense.

SUFFRAGE. We can not go into detail about the suffrage requirements of various countries. Until recent decades, almost all countries, besides limiting voting rights to men, had property owning or tax paying requirements, and some had religious requirements. Today nearly all countries have universal adult suffrage with a few limitations. There are always age and residence requirements. Convicted criminals, mental defectives, and occasionally some other categories of citizens are barred from voting. There is some variation in the voting age, though in most countries it is twenty-one. In the Soviet Union it is eighteen; in Switzerland, twenty; in Turkey, twenty-two; in Norway, twenty-three. In Italy, the age is twenty-one to vote for members of the Chamber of Deputies, but twenty-five to vote for Senators. Some other countries have individual variations. Switzerland is the only important country that has not given the vote to women.

Almost invariably, citizenship in the country is a requirement for voting. In the United States, where most suffrage regulations are left to the individual state, some states formerly allowed aliens to vote if they had taken the first step toward naturalization and met the other requirement. This is no longer true, however. In Great Britain, any British subject or citizen of the Republic of Ireland may vote if he or she has established residence. Citizens of all countries in the British Commonwealth of Nations which recognize Elizabeth II as their Queen are considered British subjects. This means that Canadians, Australians, and New Zealanders need only establish residence in Great Britain to become voters. Except the Republic of Ireland, these countries reciprocate, so that a British citizen who moves to Canada need not undergo naturalization to become a voter.

Political Parties

IMPORTANCE OF POLITICAL PARTIES. In any community as large as a nation (even a small one), political parties are necessary in the conduct of elections. They present the candidates among whom the voter must choose, and thus provide the medium through which the people secure representation.

They are also the basis for staffing and organizing the various parts of the government, particularly the legislative bodies. In some countries, especially those operating under a cabinet system, parties are the chief instrument of policy making. In other countries, though, such as the United States, Switzerland and the Scandinavian countries, their policy making role is comparatively minor. This depends on the nature of the parties, how they are organized, and the attitude of the voters toward them.

KINDS OF PARTIES. We can not undertake an exhaustive classification of political parties, but it may help us to get a clearer idea of the role of parties in various countries to take a quick look at the principal kinds. The old textbook definition of a political party was a group of voters, united by belief in certain doctrines or principles, which seeks to put its beliefs into practice by gaining control of the government through winning elections. Obviously, our major parties in the United States do not fit that definition. In many countries, though, parties of this type do exist. We may call them *doctrinal* parties, since the basis for their existence is a belief in certain doctrines or policies. Sometimes a party may form around a certain individual leader and consists of his personal following. We may call this a *leadership* party. Such was the party of General De Gaulle in France before he came to power. Such a party, of course, can not last indefinitely in that form, but with the death or retirement of the leader it may change into a different variety. Occasionally there may be formed what we may call a *coalition* party, which must be distinguished clearly from a coalition of parties. In this situation, two or more groups, which have little in common but their opposition to the party or group in power, may combine in a single party organization. These coalition parties are often effective in opposition, but usually break up when they win control of government. The old Whig Party in the United States, which operated from 1836 to 1854, was a good example.

A large class of parties, that has almost infinite variations, is the *special interest* party. Such a party may exist to serve any special interest, economic, religious, ethnic or regional. In the economic area, there are parties that claim to speak for labor, such as the Labor Party in Great Britain and the Social Democratic parties in continental Europe. There are parties that operate primarily in the interest of business, though they are apt to have a misleading name. There are also agrarian parties that exist to work for the interests of the farmers, such as the "Peasant" parties in some countries and the People's or "Populist" Party of the United States in the early 1890's. There are sometimes parties representing certain religious groups. The Center Party of pre-Hitler Germany spoke for the Catholic Church in politics, and the present day Christian Democratic Parties of West Germany, Austria and Italy have as a part of their purpose the safeguarding of religion against Communist inroads. Regional parties are not uncommon, and in countries that have several ethnic groups, each localized in a particular locality, there is usually a party to represent each such group. So long as Ireland was a part of the United Kingdom, almost all the Irish members of Parliament belonged to the Irish Nationalist Party. These varieties do not exhaust the possibility of special interest parties. For a long time in West Germany, there was a Refugee Party made up of people who had fled from Communist ruled areas.

Finally, there is the class to which our major parties belong. We may call these *institutional* parties to indicate that they have become well established institutions that are ends in themselves. One writer calls them *patronage* parties, thus suggesting that they exist only to enjoy the spoils of office, but this is hardly a fair evaluation. These parties show no clear distinction in doctrine or policies; almost every conceivable viewpoint on every public issue is to be found in each party. They do take stands in their platforms, but these stands are not consistent from one election to the next, and the platforms are usually worded so vaguely that their meaning is much in doubt. Anyway, members of the party elected to office do not feel bound by the platform. Members of Congress (or a state legislature) vote strictly as party members in organizing their respective houses, but in voting on controversial issues, the vote almost invariably cuts across party lines. These parties, as institutions, hold the loyalty of large numbers of voters who vote for the party regardless of candidates or issues, but a large segment of voters (enough to decide the outcome of elections) feel that it is more important to vote for the candidate with whose views they agree than to be guided by a party label.

OTHER CLASSIFICATIONS OF PARTIES. In two party countries, it is sometimes convenient to classify parties into *major, minor* and *third.* A major party is one with some degree of permanence (it lasts longer than an election or two) and with enough voting strength to be a real contender in national elections. In the United States, we can be sure that a national election will be won by either Republicans or Democrats; in Britain, by Conservatives or Laborites; in Canada, by Conservatives or Liberals. A minor party is one with some permanence, but without enough voting strength to have a chance of winning a national election, such as the Prohibition Party in the United States or the Liberal Party in Great Britain. A minor party may, like the British Liberals, be a former major party that has lost strength, or it may, like our Prohibitionists, have been organized to promote a cause. At least in theory, a minor party always hopes to grow into a major one. A third party is one that springs up in any one of several ways and makes a considerable show of strength for one campaign, but it does not attain permanence. It may, like Theodore Roosevelt's Progressive Party of 1912, splinter off from one of the major parties, or it may, like the Populists of the early 1890's, be organized from the ground up to voice a widespread protest against both the major parties. In multiple party countries, this classification has little meaning.

Parties may also be classified into those with open, enrolled or closed membership. In most countries with free politics, party membership is so open that anyone can become a member of any party just by deciding that he is one. He need not even vote that party's ticket consistently in elections. In some states in the United States a voter may be required to register his party for the purpose of voting in the primary election to nominate candidates, but the label does not bind him in the general election. Formerly some European parties, and some of our minor parties in America, had what we may call an enrolled membership. To become a party member, an individual had to join the party formally, pay dues, and carry a membership card; any voter, however, was eligible to join. Closed party membership is found only in one party countries where membership in *the* party carries a privileged status. In Soviet Russia, as formerly in Nazi Germany or Fascist Italy, one must be admitted to the Communist (or National Socialist or Fascist) Party, serve a period of probation, and be subject to expulsion for failure to follow the party line. Such an organization is hardly a political party at all in the sense in which we understand the term in the Free World. It is rather a closely knit oligarchy to rule the country on an authoritarian basis.

PARTY SYSTEMS. We have already spoken of countries with a one party, two party or multiple party system. In a one party system, only one party, or a group of closely affiliated parties, is permitted by law to operate. It automatically wins all elections, because there can be no opposition to its candidates. Such an arrangement is always found in totalitarian states, and may exist temporarily in other kinds of dictatorships. Where there is freedom of politics, there may be brief periods when there is only one party, as in the United States in 1820, but the voters will soon divide into a new alignment of parties.

In a two party system, there are only two major parties. There may be minor parties, which rarely affect the outcome of a national election, and from time to time third parties may disrupt the situation for one campaign. Occasionally there may be a realignment of parties, but if a country has a well established two party tradition, any departure from such an alignment will be temporary and of short duration. However, this tradition has a firm hold only in the United Kingdom and in countries that originated as British colonies. A two party alignment is sometimes approximated for a while in other countries, but not for long. The great advantage of the two party system is stability. If the "ins" go out, the "outs" come in, and there is no need to patch up coalitions to form an administration.

The normal tendency in free politics seems to be for the

voters to split up into a multiplicity of parties, setting up a party to represent every ideology and every special interest. This is the situation in most countries. It has the advantage that a voter may express his political philosophy by voting for a particular party, but it has the disadvantage of instability. Rarely will a single party win a clear cut victory in a national election, so that administrations must be formed by coalitions of parties. This predisposes to cabinet crises, and makes it difficult for an administration to follow consistent policies.

DIVISION VERSUS CONSENSUS. For free, responsible government to run smoothly there must be more agreement than disagreement among the voters, and hence among the political parties. Where disagreements run deep, involving clashes on basic principles of government, democracy is likely to break down. The victors, regarding their opponents as dangerous subversives, are apt to suppress their political enemies to the extent of destroying civil liberty. The losers, fearing for their safety, will not accept majority rule and may seek to overturn the government by force and violence. In extreme cases, this may bring about long periods of chaos and civil war. In less extreme cases, as in pre-Hitler Germany and the Fourth French Republic, it may produce a collapse of the constitutional regime. In countries where free government is stable over a long period of time, the parties may disagree on details of policy, but there is always more consensus than disagreement.

PARTY ORGANIZATION. The organizational structure of political parties not only varies from country to country, but sometimes varies among parties in the same country. The usual pattern is a pyramid of committees, beginning at the local level (in some states of the United States this is the precinct, in others, the township, and in still others, the county), rising through committees at each level of government, to a national or central committee at the top. In theory, at least, committee members at the local level are chosen by the party voters in the local area. In the United States, this is usually done in a primary election. In Britain and some other countries, it is done in what we should call a party caucus. In many countries it is done by a self-appointed group of active politicians who claim to speak for the party membership. Even in the United States and Britain, this happens to some extent behind the scenes; the politicians often make the real selections and the party voters merely ratify them. In the Soviet Union, the central committee is large and unwieldy. It designates a small subcommittee, called the "presidium" of the party (to be distinguished from the presidium of the Supreme Soviet) which manages party affairs, and hence, national affairs.

There is also, at least at the national level, a party convention of each party, usually called in Europe a party conference or a party congress. Delegates are chosen in different ways in different countries and, in the United States, in different ways in different states. In federal unions, there is also a convention in each component unit (state, *Land,* or whatever the unit may be called). In the United States, formerly, party conventions at every level from the county up nominated candidates for public offices. Now most of the states have transferred this nominating function to the primary election, and the conventions, below the national level, survive only to choose delegates to the next higher convention. As everyone knows, our national conventions, held once in four years, still nominate candidates for President and Vice President. In Europe, the national party conclave (whatever it is called) meets every year to take stands on policy, discuss party strategy, and select the national committee. It also elects a party leader who, in some cabinet governed countries, automatically becomes the party's candidate for prime minister.

In most countries, this organization is for campaign purposes only. The role of the party in government is left to the "parliamentary party," which means the organization within parliament of the members who belong to a particular party. In Britain and some other cabinet governed countries, it is the parliamentary party which selects its parliamentary leader (we should call him the floor leader in Congress or a state legislature), and it is he, rather than the leader chosen in the national convention (usually called the secretary or chief secretary of the party) who becomes the standing candidate for prime minister. In multiple party countries, it is the parliamentary party that decides how the party's members of parliament shall vote on particular issues and on votes of confidence to sustain or overthrow a prime minister and his cabinet.

In the Soviet Union there is no parliamentary party; the party presidium runs everything. In the United States there is no official distinction and members of Congress or a state legislature are tied more closely to the party committees than in most countries. In bygone times, the party caucus did direct how party members of Congress or a state legislature should vote on specific bills or other issues, but party discipline has broken down so that individual members vote as they please and the caucus rarely takes stands on issues.

NOMINATING DEVICES. The United States has the most formal nominating procedures of any important country. We are all familiar with the nomination of candidates for President and Vice President by the national conventions of the parties. Below that level, nominating procedure is left to the individual state and most of the states have provided by law for nomination in direct primaries. They differ too much from state to state for us to go into details, but in general, those voters who declare themselves adherents of each party nominate the candidates of that party directly by their votes. In the Soviet Union, nominations are made in local mass meetings and, presumably, anyone can be nominated. Actually, these meetings are stage managed so that only members of the Communist party or persons acceptable to the party organization are ever nominated. If, once in a blue moon, someone else does slip by, the Communist party committee at that level may set aside the nomination and substitute a candidate of their own choosing.

In Great Britain candidates for the House of Commons (the only national officials who are elected directly) are nominated very informally. As we have already noted, anyone may file for election and there are no party names on the ballot. Actually, however, the local committee of each party selects the person who will be that party's candidate in the constituency, and it is rare for anyone else to file. Moreover, the central committee of the party may intervene and impose a candidate, and sometimes does. The party affiliation of each candidate is played up in the campaign and, to a much greater extent than in the

United States, but to a smaller extent than on the continent of Europe, voters vote for the party rather than for the individual candidate. In this way the people are voting indirectly for prime minister, since the parliamentary leader of the party that holds a majority of the seats in the House of Commons will be appointed to that position as chief executive.

In most of the other countries of continental Europe, nominations for members of parliament and other elective officers are made by party committees at the appropriate level. In Switzerland, nominations are made in local party conventions. Nominations for members of the lower legislative chamber are usually made in the form of party lists to fit in with the arrangement for proportional representation. Except in Italy, where the voter is permitted to express the order of his preference among the names on the list, the party committee also determines the order in which candidates shall be declared elected and arranges the names on the list in that order. The voter then votes only for a party, and has no opportunity to choose among individual candidates.

PARTY RESPONSIBILITY. It is accepted theory everywhere that the party or coalition of parties which holds control of the government accepts responsibility to the voters for the conduct of government. In totalitarian states, this is a hollow sham, since the voters can not vote the party out of power. Where the separation of powers principle prevails, as in the United States, the theory does not work out very well. In the first place, it is far from uncommon for at least one house of Congress to have a majority of the other party than that of the President. In the second place, party discipline is at such a low ebb that Congressmen can not be held to a party line. Almost every important bill is passed or defeated by votes that cut across party lines. The President's party will claim credit for all legislation that appears to be popular, while the other party will try to blame the administration for any legislation to which large numbers of voters object, but this is a far cry from real party responsibility.

In most cabinet governed countries, though, the theory works out fairly well. The administration (that is, the prime minister and his cabinet) is responsible to parliament (some-times just the lower chamber, sometimes to both) and can be forced to resign by a vote of censure or failure to get a vote of confidence. On the other hand, the administration can usually bring about a dissolution of parliament and the calling of an election if it believes the voters will support its stand on an issue rather than that of the existing parliamentary majority. Under these circumstances, party members in government must stand together on issues and vote together in parliament. The voter thus looks to the party rather than to the individual statesman to get things done and can hold that party respon-sible in the next election.

INTENSITY OF PARTY BATTLES. The intensity of party conflict varies greatly from country to country, and from time to time in the same country. Until recently, in some countries outside Europe and North America, political campaigns fre-quently involved outbreaks of violence. In the United States, we make a great ado in presidential elections and an outsider might get the impression that the nation is being shaken to its foundations. Each party wants to win, to be sure; partly for the thrill of winning and partly for the patronage and other advantages that come with winning. Actually, though, no one believes that the country will be saved by the victory of one party or ruined by the victory of the other. Contrast the blood and thunder of the campaign speeches (formerly much louder than in recent campaigns) with the relative apathy of the voters as indicated by the comparatively small number who take the trouble to vote at all. In France (more so before the Fifth Republic) and Italy, party hostility runs deep, and there is much excitement, shouting and marching in the campaigns, with occasional street brawls. In Britain, the Low Countries and West Germany, party differences are more meaningful than in the United States, involving national issues more di-rectly, but campaigns are quiet affairs. In Britain, they can last only about two weeks.

In Switzerland and the Scandinavian countries, the parties are largely doctrinal in character. Each party stands for certain viewpoints. Transcending these differences, though, is broad consensus on national interests and basic national policies. There is no patronage to spur rivalry. Voters stick by their parties, so there is no "independent vote" for which to compete, and no point to bidding for the support of rival interest groups. Consequently, politics is a very calm and businesslike affair. Usually, each party nominates only candidates it is confident it can elect, so it often happens that there is only one name on the ballot for a particular position. The parties expect to work together in coalitions, and do; cabinet crises are rare.

Election Machinery

ELECTIONS. In unitary countries, elections are held under the authority of the national government; in federal unions, under the authority of the component units (states, *Länder*, cantons, provinces, or whatever they may be called). The conduct of the election and the counting of the votes are the work of some government agency, local in some countries, central in others. Usually a permanent official is in charge of counting the votes. Only in the United States is the device of bi-partisan boards used. Elections are now usually fair and honest. In times past, it was sometimes charged that the party or clique in power would always "count itself in" in every election, regardless of how the vote was cast. Also, in times past, some countries, notably Britain, spread an election over several days. Now it is the almost universal rule that an election is held on the same day throughout the country.

METHODS OF VOTING. Almost everywhere, voting is done with paper ballots, provided by the election authorities, on which the voter indicates his choice by marking an "X" for the party or candidate for whom he wishes to vote. Usually, the ballot is issued to the voter only when he appears at the polling place and, normally, provision is made for marking it in secret. Sometimes an identification mark, such as a serial number, is placed on the outside of the ballot when it is issued, to insure that there is no switching of ballots, but this mark is obliterated before the ballot is placed in the ballot box. In many urban areas in the United States, voting machines are substituted for the paper ballots, but these are not used in any other country.

In cabinet governed countries, the only names voted on in the parliamentary election are candidates for one or both chambers of the national legislative body. If the chief of state is directly elected, his election is at a different time. In federal unions other than the United States, the component units hold their elections at a different time, and almost everywhere local elections are at a different time than the parliamentary election. This means that the ballot is short and there is no problem of arrangement of names. In some of the smaller Swiss cantons, elections are held in canton-wide mass meetings, something like the old New England town meeting. Otherwise, polling places are set up in small voting districts (we call them precincts in America).

Only in the United States, where the ballot in a general election usually contains the names of candidates for two dozen or more offices, is there a problem of arranging names. This problem is met in one of two ways. About two thirds of our states use the party column ballot. Candidates' names are listed in party columns, one for each party, with the highest office to be filled at the top, the lowest at the bottom, and the others graded in between. There is a circle at the head of the column in which the voter may mark an "X" to vote a "straight" party ticket, but there is also a square beside each name for the voter who prefers to vote for individual candidates. The other states use the office block type of ballot on which all candidates for one office are grouped together. This form of ballot usually provides no short cut for straight party voting.

Countries with a high percentage of illiteracy use party emblems which the illiterate voter can recognize if he can not read the party name. Some states in the United States retain the party emblems on the ballot as a matter of tradition. India, where most voters are illiterate, has an interesting scheme. In each precinct, a ballot box is provided for each party, marked with the party emblem. The voter is given a marble instead of the usual paper ballot, and he deposits this marble in the box of the party of his choice.

Where party lists are used for proportional representation,

the voter ordinarily can vote only for the party of his choice with no selection of individual candidates. A square or circle is provided under the party name and emblem in which he marks an "X" to indicate his vote. As we have already noted, though, Italy and some of the smaller countries permit the voter to indicate his preference among names on the list as well as to vote for a party. In the Italian plan, the voter marks an "X" for a party, which he can recognize by the party emblem. In addition, if he is literate and cares to do so, he may indicate, by writing names from the list of that party in the order in which he prefers the candidates to be selected in filling the party's quota of Deputies in parliament, and the averages of these preferences are followed in declaring candidates elected.

SAFEGUARDING THE VOTER. Everywhere in the Free World there are laws to prevent the intimidation of voters, but in some politically immature countries such intimidation does occur. Likewise, the Free World countries all have laws for secrecy in voting, but the arrangements provided for securing it vary in effectiveness. In most countries with responsible governments, though, secrecy of the ballot is safeguarded quite effectively. In totalitarian countries and other dictatorships, ballot secrecy is either a sham or does not exist, since real secrecy would encourage voting against the official lists. Many countries, including most of the states of the United States, permit official party watchers in the polling places to guard against fraud.

Periodic Versus "Called" Elections

PERIODIC ELECTIONS. In countries like the United States and Switzerland, where the separation of powers principle is followed, all elections are held on a regular schedule. The only "called" elections are to fill vacancies. In countries where the dissolution of parliament is possible, members of the legislative body are chosen for maximum terms (usually different for the two chambers) and, if there has not been a dissolution by the end of that term, an election is held at that time. Under present constitutions, no major country elects its chief of state directly (although the United States comes close to doing so), but when some of them did, and in less important countries that still do, he is elected for a fixed term and an election is held near the end of his term.

CALLED ELECTIONS. In most countries, elections in individual constituencies can be called to fill vacancies, and sometimes on a wider scale to vote on questions in a referendum or plebiscite. We are concerned here, though, with called general elections. Except under revolutionary conditions, such elections occur only in countries where a dissolution of parliament is possible. The constitution usually provides that, at the time of a dissolution, the chief of state shall call an election within a specified number of days. In Britain, custom decrees that the interval between a dissolution and an election be not more than three weeks. The French constitution provides not less than twenty nor more than forty days. Other countries have similar short limits. In Britain, Parliament may, in national emergencies, extend its own term, and did so during both world wars. Britain also has the tradition that a Parliament shall never be permitted to expire by limitation. A few weeks before the legal end of the terms of members of the House of Commons, the Prime Minister always has the monarch dissolve Parliament.

MERITS OF THE TWO. The chief merit of regular elections is that everyone knows when an election is coming and can prepare accordingly. There is the disadvantage that, if an election falls due in the midst of a great war or other national crisis, the election can not be postponed to calmer times. The uncertainty preceding the election may hamper the government greatly in dealing with critical situations, and the election itself may result in "changing horses in the middle of the stream," as Lincoln put it. There is also the disadvantage, especially in the United States, but to some extent also in other countries, that great issues do not usually arise to fit an election schedule. Artificial issues are then raised for campaign purposes, but they confuse the voter rather than guide him.

On the other hand, a dissolution is usually the result of a clash on issues, so that the election called at that particular time gives the voters a chance to settle the issues by their votes. It amounts to a referendum, though the actual vote is for legislators who support or oppose the position taken by the cabinet on the issue.

INITIATIVE AND REFERENDUM. In Switzerland and some of the states of the United States, the voters may legislate directly through the initiative and referendum. The initiative is an arrangement by which, upon presentation of a petition signed by a specified number of voters, a measure of legislation is submitted to the voters in a regular or called election. If approved by a majority of those voting on it, it becomes law. In the referendum, a bill which has passed (or in some cases, failed to pass) the legislative body is submitted to the voters for approval or disapproval. In Switzerland, and the American states that use the scheme, a petition similar to the initiative petition is presented asking that a bill that has passed the legislative body be submitted to the voters. When such a petition is filed, the act does not become law until the voters have had a chance to approve or reject it in a general or called election. This amounts to a popular veto on legislative acts.

Much the same arrangement for the referendum exists in Italy with the additional feature that in some situations a referendum may be had on a bill that has failed to pass parliament. In the Fifth French Republic, the President may order a referendum on bills for the reorganization of government machinery or involving some treaty commitments.

Suggested Questions for Discussion

1. How important are suffrage regulations in providing representation of the people in parliament? What is more important?
2. Compare the principal bases of representation (single member districts, party lists and proportional representation). In what situation is each the most advantageous?
3. Compare the essential characteristics of political parties in: (1) the United States, (2) Great Britain, (3) France, and (4) the Soviet Union.

4. Compare the good and bad features of different kinds of political parties (institutional, doctrinal, special interest, etc.).
5. Compare the good and bad features of one-party, two-party and multiple-party systems.
6. To what extent is it desirable that contending political parties agree or disagree on major policy issues?
7. Under what conditions does party responsibility work best?
8. Compare the merits of the methods of nominating party candidates for the national legislative body used in: (1) the United States, (2) Great Britain and (3) most countries of continental Europe.
9. What are the comparative advantages and disadvantages of periodic and called elections?
10. Compare the main features of party organization in: (1) the United States, (2) Great Britain, (3) western continental Europe and (4) the Soviet Union.
11. Are political parties necessary in modern government? If so, why?
12. Compare the desirability of party regularity by the voter and independent voting.

Bibliography

Bailey, S., Ed., Political Parties and Party Systems in Britain (New York, 1952)

Barron, R. W., Parties and Politics in Modern France (Washington, D. C., 1959)

Butler, D. E., Ed., Elections Abroad (London, 1959)

Duverger, M., Political Parties: Their Organization and Activity in the Modern State (New York, 1954)

Macridis, R. C., and Brown, B. E., Comparative Politics (Homewood, Ill., 1961)

Meyer, E. W., Political Parties in Western Germany (Library of Congress, 1951)

Middleton, Wilfrid, The French Political System (New York, 1933)

Neumann, S., Ed., Modern Political Parties (University of Chicago, 1956)

Nicolson, N., People and Parliament (London, 1958)

Soltau, R. H., French Parties and Politics, 1871-1930 (New York, 1930)

Williams, P., Politics in Post-War France (New York, 1954)

FIVE

The Executive Branch

Chief of State and Head of Government

THE DISTINCTION. It will help in getting a clearer understanding of some aspects of the executive branch in many countries to distinguish between the chief of state and the head of government. We seldom make this distinction in the United States because our President and the governors of our states combine both roles in the same person. It is possible, though, to apply the distinction to their functions. In most cabinet governed countries, the chief of state and the head of government are different persons, each with his own role to play. As we shall see more fully later, the distinction becomes somewhat hazy in the Fifth French Republic.

THE CHIEF OF STATE. The chief of state is the ceremonial head of the nation and personifies the national sovereignty. Treaties are made, and all executive orders and decrees are issued in his name. In form, he appoints all appointive officers, is commander-in-chief of the armed forces, and possesses a wide range of "prerogative" powers, including the power to dissolve parliament and call elections. There are certain formal functions he must perform, such as accrediting and receiving ambassadors and commissioning all officers, civil and military. He must also perform many functions which custom decrees, such as greeting visiting dignitaries, visiting distressed areas, presiding at some public gatherings, sending letters of condolence or felicitation (as occasion may require) to other chiefs of state, and do a miscellaneous assortment of other things. In any matter that involves discretion or public policy, he acts only on the advice of his ministers, who assume responsibility for his acts. He may sometimes exert some influence on public policy by "advising his advisers," but usually he merely acts as they direct.

The chief of state may be a hereditary monarch or an elective official, usually called a president. This may make considerable difference in the ceremony that surrounds him and the respect paid to him, but it makes no difference in his real power. It is sometimes said that the chief of state is the person to whom the prime minister and his cabinet resign. When a resignation occurs, the chief of state, at least in form, appoints the new prime minister. In multiple party countries, he may have some latitude in deciding what party leader he will ask to "form a government" (become prime minister), but he will have to accept one who can put together a coalition that can get a vote of confidence in parliament. In two party countries, the chief of state must appoint as prime minister the leader of the party that wins a majority of seats in parliament.

Vacancies in the position of chief of state are provided for in different ways. If a monarch dies, abdicates or is deposed, the heir to the throne assumes the post immediately. If the monarch is a child, or if an adult monarch is incapacitated, a regent or council of regency is set up to perform the functions of the office. If a president dies, resigns or is removed before the end of his term, there is usually a stand-by official to take over his functions, at least temporarily. In the United States and some other countries, there is the Vice President who fills out the unexpired term. In France, the President of the Senate acts until an election can be held to fill the vacancy. In West Germany, the President of the *Bundesrat* acts similarly, as does the President of the Senate in Italy. Several smaller countries provide that the chief justice of the highest court shall become acting president.

THE HEAD OF GOVERNMENT. The head of government is the real chief executive. Either as an individual or with the collaboration of cabinet colleagues, he directs most government activities and makes top policy decisions. In cabinet governed countries, he is the prime minister. As such, along with his strictly executive functions, he and his cabinet colleagues have an important part in legislation. In most countries that operate under a cabinet system, the prime minister and members of his cabinet are members of the legislative body, and act as a steering committee to prepare most important legislation and steer it through parliament. In countries where they are not members, such as France and West Germany, they have access to the lower chamber and can take part in its debates. Hence, the prime minister may be considered not only chief executive, but chief legislator also. Often he may, through the chief of state, issue decrees or executive orders that have the force of law.

Single and Plural Executives

SINGLE EXECUTIVES. In the United States government and the governments of other countries (mostly in Latin America) that have copied our system, all executive power is concentrated in one person, the President. For that reason, this plan of government is sometimes called the "presidential system" in distinction from the "cabinet system." There are other executive officers, to be sure, but they are subordinates of the President and are subject to his control and direction. He appoints them (in our case, with the consent of the Senate) and may dismiss them. He has the final responsibility for all policy decisions. He has less control over the legislative body than does a prime minister, but he is still expected to exercise legislative leadership.

TYPES OF PLURAL EXECUTIVES. The term "plural executive" means only that all executive power is not concentrated in a single individual, but that leaves room for a great deal of variation. Most of the states of the United States have plural executives of a sort. There are several other executive officers elected independently of the governor, and over whom the governor has no control. This is not the collective executive that we usually think of when we speak of a "plural" executive, and its main effect is to restrict the powers of the governor.

Vesting the executive power in a board or council is not usually satisfactory because of the frequent need for quick decisions. Our constitutional convention of 1787 considered this device and rejected it. The French tried it in their Directory of 1795-1799, but it was a dismal failure, partly because of the personnel of the Directory. The only country that uses it today, and with general success, is Switzerland. The Swiss Federal Council consists of seven councillors elected by the two chambers of the legislative body meeting jointly, for concurrent four year terms. The Council as a body has the usual executive powers. The legislators also elect one of the councillors as president and also one as vice-president. This President of the Federal Council is sometimes called President of the Swiss Confederation, because he represents the nation on ceremonial occasions. He is not, however, a chief of state. Nor is he a prime minister; he neither selects his colleagues nor has any special relationship with the legislature. He presides at meetings of the Council, but he has only the same vote as other members. The Council sometimes delegates special chores to him, but in performing them he is acting only as a one man committee of the Council.

THE CABINET AS EXECUTIVE. The most widely used form of plural executive is the cabinet. The prime minister is appointed by the chief of state, though the choice is dictated by the party situation in the legislative body. The prime minister then selects his fellow ministers and they, in turn, are formally appointed by the chief of state. In some countries, either prior to or immediately following this formal appointment, the prime minister designate must get a vote of approval of the make-up of his cabinet from the legislative body (in most countries, only from the lower chamber).

The cabinet as a body is a collective executive. The prime minister is expected to *lead* the cabinet as well as preside at its meetings, but he should take no action without the consent of his colleagues. Each minister normally heads a department and may make departmental decisions somewhat independently. However, if a decision involves general policy, the minister must have the approval of his colleagues and of the prime minister, since the entire cabinet is responsible to parliament for any act of any member. There has been a growing tendency in recent decades for the relationship of the prime minister to his colleagues to change into something resembling the relationship of our President to his so-called cabinet. He sometimes acts without first consulting his colleagues, but if they demand a voice in a decision, he is still bound to follow their collective judgment.

National Variations

VARIATIONS IN THE PATTERN. What we have been saying is in the nature of generalizations. Actually no two cabinet governed countries are exactly alike in their arrangements. Three of the major countries deviate from this generalized pattern sufficiently to justify brief individual treatment.

GREAT BRITAIN. Great Britain was the original home of the cabinet system, but the present scheme is the product of long evolution, and it is still evolving. Two institutions that existed before the cabinet developed still survive to complicate the picture. In Britain, the ministry is much more inclusive than the cabinet. All department heads and sub-heads and the heads of many administrative agencies are considered ministers. So is the Lord Chancellor. So, too, are the parliamentary undersecretaries, whose only function is as spokesmen for their departments in the other house of Parliament than the one of which the department head is a member. The cabinet consists of those ministers, the number varying from time to time, who are selected by the Prime Minister to act as a consultative group for making policy decisions. The whole ministry, however, is responsible to the House of Commons. If the prime minister is forced to resign by opposition in Parliament, the whole ministry goes out with him. The privy council was originally a group of royal advisers whom the King consulted in person. In Tudor and Stuart times, it was a very important organ of government. Today it survives only as a shadow. It has several hundred members, former cabinet ministers (once a member always a member) and other persons who have been given the title of Privy Councillor as an honor. As a government organ, it consists of a few cabinet members (three are a quorum) meeting with the Lord President of the Council. It has the power to "advise" the King or Queen to issue "orders in council" which have the force of law, but these orders may be overruled by Parliament.

Otherwise, the British cabinet system is about as one would expect in a two party country. The entire ministry is made up of adherents of the prime minister's party, which is the party with a majority of the members of the House of Commons. The prime minister may occasionally shift a minister from one post to another, or pressure one into resigning. A change of ministry rarely occurs, though, except when a general election changes the party majority in Commons. Back in the 1920's, when the rise of the Labor Party and the decline of the Liberal Party were both in midstream, there was a period when none of the three parties held a majority in Commons. There were then several changes of ministry in relatively rapid succession.

A term used in connection with the British executive that sometimes baffles Americans is "the Crown." It will serve very well for our purpose to think of the Crown as the whole executive branch of the British government. To Britains, it means the monarch in his or her official capacity. Thus, when they speak of Crown property, they mean what we should call national or public property, as distinct from property the monarch may own personally. The powers of the Crown are still, technically, the powers of the monarch, but since the monarch exercises these powers only on the advice of ministers, we may think of them as executive powers.

FRANCE. The French cabinet is called the *government* in the constitution. In popular usage, the cabinet is often referred to as "the government" in other countries as well. The prime minister (called officially the *premier*) is appointed by the President of the Republic and his appointment need not be confirmed by parliament. He, in consultation with the President, selects the other ministers. Ministers may not be members of either chamber of parliament, but they have access to both chambers with the right to participate in debate. The "government" as a group, may also introduce bills into either chamber, and these have priority of consideration as do government bills in the British Parliament.

The government is declared by the constitution to be responsible to the National Assembly. However, a motion for a vote of censure, which if passed would force the resignation of the ministers, must be signed by one tenth of the members of the Assembly, and a vote of confidence can be taken only if initiated by the premier. This is intended to prevent the frequent cabinet crises that plagued the Third and Fourth Republics.

The most distinctive feature of the French executive branch is the position of the President of the Republic. The constitution tried to find a middle ground between the American presidential system and the old cabinet system to which the French people were accustomed. It is an open secret that the office was tailored to the ideas of General De Gaulle who, it was taken for granted, would be the first President. Certainly the French President today is a far cry from the mere ceremonial chief of state of the Third and Fourth Republics. He selects the premier quite independently of parliament and could force his resignation at any time. He takes the initiative in issuing decree laws (though he must have the consent of the premier and the presidents of the two assemblies). He can, on his own initiative, dissolve parliament at any time, so long as he does not do so twice within a year. He presides over the meetings of the cabinet.

Under the original provision of the constitution, he was elected for a seven year term by a huge electoral college consisting of members of both chambers of Parliament, together with mayors, deputy mayors and municipal councillors of the communes. This was intended to free the President both from party politics and from control by Parliament. However, on October 28, 1962, the voters of France, in a special referendum election, approved a constitutional amendment, submitted by President De Gaulle, which provides for direct popular election of the President. While he is not quite the supreme single executive that the President of the United States is, he approximates it rather closely.

WEST GERMANY. The President of the German Federal Republic is a ceremonial chief of state elected for a five year term by a convention which consists of all the members of the *Bundestag* plus delegates from the lower houses of the state legislatures. He does not have the emergency powers held by the president under the Weimar Republic. About his only discretionary power is that, if the *Bundestag* elects a chancellor by a plurality vote, the President may either accept him or dissolve the *Bundestag*. When the chancellorship is vacant, the President appoints a chancellor who must be approved by the *Bundestag*. This means he has no real choice, since he must always appoint the man who has the votes in the *Bundestag* to assure confirmation.

The chancellor is much more an independent executive. His powers are far greater than those of a typical prime minister. He appoints his cabinet members with no requirement of legislative confirmation; they are responsible to him alone, and he can remove them at will. He is technically responsible to the *Bundestag*, but under such restrictions, already noted, that this is almost meaningless. Even the failure of Chancellor Adenauer's Christian Democratic Party to secure a majority of the *Bundestag* in the 1961 election failed to dislodge the chancellor, though he did have to make some deals with a minor party in order to remain in office. We have already noticed some of the West German chancellor's unusual powers. Like a prime minister, he can introduce legislation, even though he is not a member of either house, and he can address either house at any time. Not only does he submit the budget, but if parliament fails to pass it, he can continue the budget of the preceding year, collecting the revenues and authorizing expenditures. He can veto any increase the parliament may make in any item in his budget. He formulates and executes all executive policies. So long as he can maintain a parliamentary majority, either through his own party or through a coalition with a minor party, his legislative program is assured of enactment. If the *Bundestag* should defeat one of his measures, he can declare a state of "legislative emergency," and the bill can be enacted by the *Bundesrat* alone; however, he can do this for only six months during his term of office. If the *Bundestag* tries to pass a vote of censure, but upholds the chancellor by less than an absolute majority, he may have the President dissolve the *Bundestag* and call an election. All in all, the chancellor is an even more independent executive than is the President of the United States.

Executive Powers and Functions

WHAT ARE EXECUTIVE POWERS? The general nature and scope of executive powers should be apparent from what has already been said, but, at the risk of repetition, it may be helpful to summarize some of the powers and functions that are distinctly executive and the major areas of executive activity. Most of the powers can be grouped under three headings: policy making, the appointing power, and discretionary or prerogative powers.

POLICY MAKING. The function of formulating all government policies that are not covered by legislation, and of carrying into effect both these policies and those embodied in legislative acts, belongs to the executive. Of course, much of the policy making must be delegated to subordinates, but the responsibility and the need for making final decisions in difficult situations rest with the top executive, whether that top executive be a single individual like our President, a cabinet, or a body like the Swiss Federal Council. Most of the execution of policy must likewise be delegated. This involves administration, which we shall discuss in the next chapter. In this matter, too, responsibility is at the top, so the executive must issue directives, set up administrative policy, and require reports. It is often said that the main work of an executive is making decisions.

THE APPOINTING POWER. In almost all countries, all national officers except legislators and the chief of state, are appointed by the executive. If there is a separate chief of state, it is he (or she) who has the formal appointing power, but it is the ministers who "advise" (and so control) the appointments. Heads of departments sometimes select their own subordinates, but not always. In the United States, undersecretaries and assistant secretaries are appointed by the President. Officials below the policy making level are usually selected under a merit system, but must receive formal appointments from the executive or chief of state.

The appointing power is a vital instrument in formulating and executing policy. The top executive can not possibly work out all the details of policy in a particular area of government or directly supervise the application of details of policy. It is vital, then, that the executive be able to select subordinates in whom he has confidence to manage these details. Political party considerations usually play a part in appointments. In times past, this often meant that the "patronage" (making appointments to pay political debts) deteriorated into a corrupt spoils system, but in most countries this situation has been remedied by the adoption of a merit system for most government employees. In multiple party countries, the appointive positions must be apportioned among the parties that make up the government coalition, roughly in proportion to their voting strength in parliament. In two party countries (except for some agencies which the law requires to be bipartisan) appointments normally go to adherents of the party in power.

DISCRETIONARY POWERS. The executive always has some powers which he (or they) can exercise at discretion. In Britain, these are called "prerogative powers" because they are the historic "prerogatives of the Crown," which the monarch now exercises on the advice of ministers. One of these is the pardoning power. Another is the power, in certain circumstances, to issue proclamations that have the force of law. In the United States, these are called "executive orders"; in Britain, "orders in council"; in France, "decree laws" or "ordinances." Other countries have other names for them. Unless specifically authorized by the constitution or by law, such orders are usually subject to a veto by the legislative body. In the United States and Britain, such orders take effect immediately, but may be disallowed by the legislative body (Congress or Parliament) within sixty days or, if not in session, within sixty days of the opening of the next session. In France, a legislative act ruled by the Constitutional Council to be regulatory in character may be modified by presidential decree approved by the premier.

In cabinet governed countries, the executive normally has the power to dissolve parliament (or perhaps, just the lower chamber) and call an election. Where there is a separate chief of state, he issues the formal orders for the dissolution and election, but he does this on the advice of the prime minister. Even in France, where the President may order a dissolution on his own initiative, he must consult the premier, but this is a mere formality.

Areas of Executive Activity

DIVERSITY OF ACTIVITIES. The areas of governmental activity in which the executive has powers or functions are too numerous to list completely. Just to give an idea of the diversity of executive responsibilities, though, we may glance at half a dozen of the more important areas. These are foreign relations, military affairs, legislative matters, financial management, ceremonial functions, and administration.

FOREIGN RELATIONS. The conduct of foreign relations is always a function of the executive. They are conducted in the name of the chief of state, who always has certain formalities to perform in this connection such as receiving ambassadors and entertaining visiting chiefs of state. If, like our President, he is also head of government, he makes foreign policy decisions. Otherwise they are made for him by the working executive. The routine work of handling foreign affairs, including the making of some policy decisions, is vested in a department head usually called the foreign minister (in our case, Secretary of State). He gives directions to his country's ambassadors and other representatives to foreign countries, and receives their reports. He confers with ambassadors or other representatives of other countries accredited to his own country. He conducts negotiations, either in person or through diplomatic representatives. From time to time, he attends foreign ministers' conferences, either in connection with international organizations such as NATO and the OAS, or special meetings of foreign ministers called for a special purpose. He keeps the head of government informed of all diplomatic developments and consults with him on matters of policy; if there is any disagreement, the foreign minister always defers to the judgment of the head of government.

MILITARY AFFAIRS. The chief of state is always the nominal commander-in-chief of the nation's armed forces, but unless he is also head of government, the actual management of all non-technical military matters falls to the working executive. There is always a cabinet department of defense (or something analogous to it) whose head is normally a civilian. The English speaking nations first adopted the principle that military power should be subject to civilian control to prevent the rise of military dictatorship. Most of the more important countries now follow this rule, though in some governments outside Europe and North America, a military man may sometimes hold this post. Everywhere, of course, technical military matters are left to officers in uniform. Especially in a cabinet system, the defense minister may have a fairly free hand in managing his department, subject to the willingness of the legislative body to provide the funds he needs. Under present world conditions, though, it is necessary for the head of government to take a major role in military affairs. Several times during World War II there were "summit conferences" of heads of government to plan Allied strategy. Military power and its disposition are also major factors in diplomacy, so that a head of government must take them into account in directing foreign relations. This is especially true under "cold war" conditions.

There is even more to it than that. The commander-in-chief, on his own or on the "advice" of the head of government, appoints the military officers and can discipline or remove them. He may issue direct orders to the forces, as when President Truman ordered United States troops into action in Korea. In time of war he may exercise some arbitrary powers over the civilian population on the ground that such action is necessary to the war effort. It was in his role of commander-in-chief that President Lincoln issued the emancipation proclamation. Certainly, this is one of the most important areas of executive activity.

LEGISLATIVE MATTERS. The executive is always a part of the legislative machinery. In the United States, the President recommends legislation in his messages, pushes for its enactment by informal means, and may veto an act of Congress of which he disapproves. Although the veto is in abeyance in Britain, where it originated, many countries besides the United States still use it. In cabinet governed countries the connection is even closer. Normally the prime minister and his cabinet members are also members of parliament. As such, they are a steering committee that introduces most important legislation and pilots it through to adoption; if parliament rejects their proposals, it means either a resignation of the cabinet or a dissolution of parliament. Even in France and West Germany, where the ministers are not members of parliament, the pressure the executive can exert on the legislative body is stronger than in the United States. We have already noted the ways in which this is true.

The executive may also have what we may call delegated legislative power. The French constitution provides that the cabinet may ask parliament for authority, for a limited time, to issue "ordinances" that have the force of law. In Britain it is fairly common for Parliament (on motion of a minister) to grant broad advance authority to issue orders in council. On many occasions, our Congress has delegated to the President the power to legislate on certain matters by proclamation. Our supreme court has held that this practice is constitutional so long as the congressional act conferring the power sets limitations of the President's discretion.

FINANCIAL MANAGEMENT. The executive always shares with the legislative body in the management of national government finance. With such minor exceptions as that noted for West Germany, the power to levy taxes, authorize borrowing, and appropriate money belongs exclusively to the legislative body. All important countries, however, have adopted a budget system which requires the executive to prepare a budget, with estimates of income and recommendations of expenditures, which is submitted to parliament. In the United States, the budget is prepared for the President by a budget director and his staff, but the President scrutinizes and sometimes changes it before sending it to Congress. In Britain, it is prepared by the Chancellor of the Exchequer, who corresponds roughly to our Secretary of the Treasury, but the whole cabinet passes on it before it is presented in Parliament. In most countries, the budget is prepared by the finance minister. In the United States, Congress may increase, decrease or eliminate items in the budget and, unless he is willing to veto an appropriation bill providing the working funds for several departments or agencies, the President must accept what Congress gives him. In some of our states, the governor may veto individual items in appropriation bills, and in a few of them may even reduce the amount of an appropriation, but the President does not have this power. In most European countries, parliament must accept or reject the budget entire. If a committee of parliament thinks an item should be changed, the head of that committee confers with the finance minister and tries to persuade him to make the change. In most cabinet governed countries rejection of the budget is regarded as a vote of censure and requires either the resignation of the ministry or the dissolution of parliament. This is not true in France, West Germany or Switzerland, but they do not have typical cabinet systems.

CEREMONIAL FUNCTIONS. Where the chief of state and the head of government are the same person, as in the case of our President, he has to perform all of the ceremonial functions that have been mentioned as falling to the chief of state. Where there is no real chief of state, some official, such as the President of the Presidium in the Soviet Union or the President of the Federal Council in Switzerland, is desig-

Relation of Executive and Legislative Branches
Presidential System—United States
SEPARATION OF POWERS

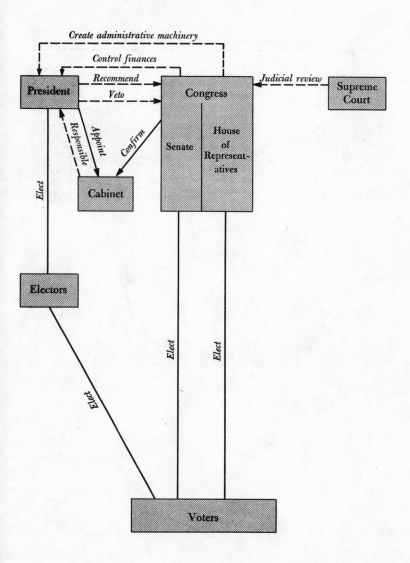

Relation of Executive and Legislative Branches
Cabinet System—Great Britain

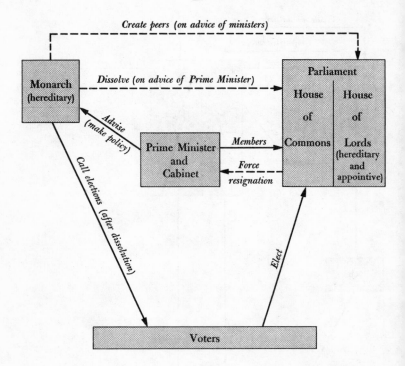

Relation of Executive and Legislative Branches
Mixed System—France
FIFTH REPUBLIC

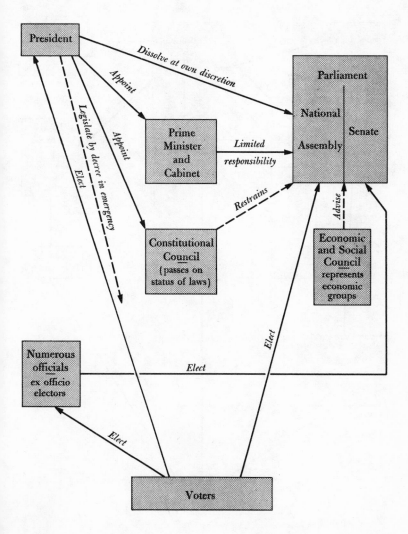

Relation of Executive and Legislative Branches
Chancellor System—West Germany

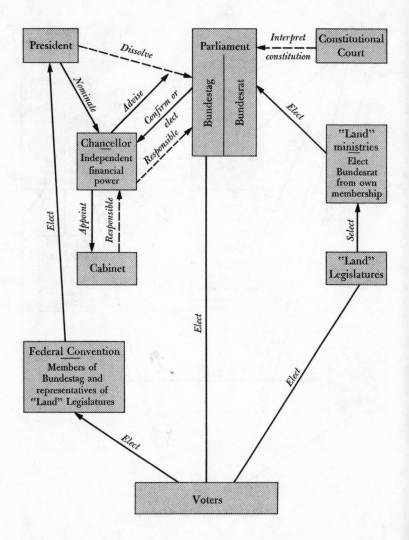

Relation of Executive and Legislative Branches
Soviet System—U.S.S.R.

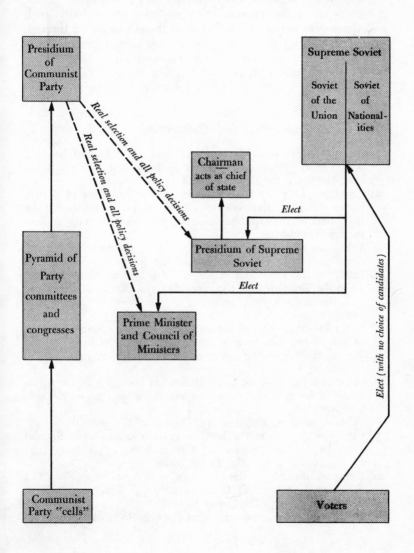

nated to do the strictly ceremonial chores. Even where there is a separate head of government, though, that official does not escape all ceremonial responsibilities. He must greet visiting heads of other governments and must make public speeches on some ceremonial occasions. He usually feels called upon to maintain contact with the press, either through press conferences or by some other means. He has other responsibilities, which are largely ceremonial, as the official leader of his political party. All of these things take time and energy that he could use better for other activities.

Suggested Questions for Discussion

1. Analyze the distinction between chief of state and head of government. Why is the distinction important in some countries, but not in the United States?
2. Compare the position and powers of the President of France under the Fifth Republic with those of presidents under the third and fourth republics and the presidents of most cabinet governed countries.
3. What are the principal types of plural executives? What are some distinctive characteristics of the Swiss executive?
4. Compare the position and powers of a typical prime minister (e.g. the British) with those of: (1) the American President, (2) the French Premier and (3) the West German Chancellor.
5. What are some typical limitations in various countries on the power of the executive to make and execute national policy.
6. Why is the appointing power one of the most important executive powers?
7. Why can the head of government not delegate his responsibility in foreign relations to the extent he can in other executive areas?
8. What is involved in the military power of the executive?
9. Compare the role of the head of government in legislation in: (1) the United States, (2) Great Britain, (3) Italy, (4) Switzerland and (5) the Soviet Union.
10. Compare the role of the executive in national finance in: (1) the United States, (2) Great Britain, (3) France, (4) West Germany and (5) the Soviet Union.
11. How may the executive be held responsible to the people in:

(1) the United States, (2) Great Britain, (3) France, (4) West Germany and (5) the Soviet Union?
12. What are the advantages of retaining the forms of monarchy in the European countries that do so?

Bibliography

Baker, Sir Ernest, British Constitutional Monarchy (London, 1955)

Carter, Byrun E., The Office of Prime Minister (Princeton University, 1956)

Jennings, W. I., Cabinet Government (New York, 1959)

Keith, A. B., The British Cabinet System (London, 1952)

Martin, K., The Magic of Monarchy (New York, 1937)

Wiseman, H. V., Cabinet in the Commonwealth (New York, 1958)

Administration

Meaning and Importance of Administration

WHAT IS ADMINISTRATION? A word of many meanings, administration may be thought of, for present purposes, as getting the work of government done. The term is also applied to the organizational machinery used to get this work done. When the Constitution of the United States declares that the President "shall take care that the laws be faithfully executed," it is making him chief administrator. We are apt to think of this constitutional provision as referring to what we commonly call law enforcement: that is, enforcing the laws that define and prescribe the punishment of crimes. It does include some phases of that, though law enforcement, in this sense, is mainly the function of the courts. But only a small portion of our laws, or those of any other country, are of this kind. Most of them are setting up tasks for government to do and providing the agencies to get these tasks done. All of this administrative machinery is part of the executive branch of government.

IMPORTANCE. The importance of administration becomes apparent when we think of the enormous variety of things that governments do. First of all, there are "housekeeping" chores: collecting the taxes and other revenues, checking on expenditures, hiring and managing employees, taking the census, and caring for and managing government property. There are a wide variety of service activities, such as forecasting the weather, conserving natural resources, and constructing and managing reclamation projects. Governments regulate many types of business activities in the public interest and often regulate labor relations. To a different extent in different countries, government itself engages in business enterprises. The government always operates the post office. In many countries, it operates the railroads, telephone and telegraph service, and broadcasting. In some countries, such as Great Britain, the government operates other major business enterprises, as electric power and coal mining. In Communist countries, the government operates all business. Most governments also provide and administer various projects in the aid of public welfare, such as social security, public housing, and, in Great Britain and the Communist countries, medical care.

To do all these things with reasonable efficiency, specialized agencies must be organized and staffed, coordinated into a workable system, directed and supervised. This is administration.

Organization of Administration

ADMINISTRATIVE AGENCIES. An officer or group of officers charged with the performance of one of these 'tasks is called an administrative agency. In a large agency like the Post Office Department, there may be hundreds of subordinate officers and hundreds of thousands of employees. The headquarters of an agency is usually in the national capital, but there are apt to be offices or branches scattered over the entire country. In a federal union, each of the component units has its own administrative organization separate from the federal.

In the United States government, administrative agencies are grouped into three classes according to their relationship to the executive. First, there are those that make up the Executive Office of the President: the Bureau of the Budget, the Council of Economic Advisers, the National Security Council, the Office of Defense Mobilization, and the White House Office. These are under the President's personal direction. Second are the Departmental Agencies. These are all that come under the cabinet departments. They are responsible to the President through the respective department heads. Finally, there is a large group called Independent Agencies. They differ greatly in the actual amount of independence they enjoy. About their only common characteristic is that they are not in any of the cabinet departments. Something approximating such a grouping is found in most countries, though usually a larger proportion of the agencies are under the authority of a minister or department head.

TYPES OF AGENCIES. There are several types of agency organization, each best adapted to a particular kind of work. The single administrator, or single headed agency, is best suited to tasks that involve little or no discretion or policy making. In the United States government, all departmental agencies are of this type, but this is not true in all countries. The board or commission (plural headed agency) is to be preferred where much of the work involves making decisions or issuing regulations. With the exception of the post office, agencies that either operate or regulate business are apt to be of this type. Variations of these are the board or commission to make decisions with a single administrator under its direction, and the single administrator with an advisory board. Still another type is the government corporation. Though entirely government owned, it has the usual corporate powers to hold property, buy and sell, sue and be sued. It is used to some extent in the United States, and more extensively in Great Britain, to carry on government business enterprises.

DEGREES OF CENTRALIZATION. In different countries the control and direction of administrative processes are centralized or decentralized in varying degrees. In federal unions, the component units always have their own administrative machinery that is largely independent of control by the central or federal government. When the matter administered overlaps, the federal authority prevails over that of the unit (state, *Land,* province or canton) in case of conflict. Within the unit itself, administration may be centralized under the unit government, or much discretion may be left to administrative authorities in the subdivisions, such as counties and cities. In unitary states, administrative control may be largely decentralized, as it is in Great Britain, where much latitude is left to municipal and county authorities, or highly centralized as it is in France where almost all administrative decisions are made by a ministry in Paris.

In a very large country, too much centralization has its disadvantages in trying to impose uniform regulations and procedures on very diverse areas. The Soviet Union has had this experience. Nominally federal, but actually unitary, and with all industry state enterprise, the Russians tried to have everything administered from Moscow. Under Khrushchev, however, they have begun decentralizing control in regional authorities. These are bound, of course, by Communist Party pronouncements, but at least they can make local adjustments and adaptations to fit conditions in their respective regions.

The Civil Service

CIVIL SERVICE AND THE MERIT SYSTEM. Civil service means simply working for a government — any government. The term is also used to mean the government employees themselves, and the arrangements for recruiting, promoting and protecting them, and it is in this sense that we speak of a country's civil service. If a person is working for the government, he is in the civil service, whether he gets his job through a spoils system, a merit system, or no system at all. Today, almost all of the important countries have adopted some kind of merit system for most of their employees. Details vary so greatly that we shall need to look at several countries separately, but a few generalizations may be in order. Employees are selected initially on the basis of merit, usually determined by competitive examinations. Promotions are usually based mainly on service records, though further examinations may also be required for promotion. The employee is protected against dismissal for reasons of party politics or the favoritism of superiors, and usually may retire on a pension after a long period of service. In the United States and Great Britain, the civil servants are forbidden, for their own protection, to take an active part in politics.

WHO ARE INCLUDED. Political officials are never under the merit system and are not regarded as included in the civil service. In France, however, the line is very hazy. In the United States, temporary and casual workers, and workers on construction projects, are not included. In Britain, employees of the government corporations which operate the nationalized industries, and employees of the nationalized industries in France, are not treated as being a part of the civil service, though they are given some protection in their employment.

BUREAUCRACY. Another term often used in connection with the civil service is bureaucracy. Literally it means government by bureaus, but it is often used to mean the body of civil servants, emphasizing the important role they play in carrying on government and their influence on government policies. In the United States and Britain, the word is generally used as a term of opprobrium, insinuating that the civil servants have far more influence in government than they ought to have. The term also carries the implication that the civil servants, or at least the higher ranks of them, constitute a privileged class. In Britain and France, these positions do confer social status on their holders, but it is only in West Germany and the Soviet Union, which has no merit system, that the administrators are a real bureaucracy.

LABOR RELATIONS OF CIVIL SERVANTS. In the United States, Britain and France, government employees may have their own unions affiliated with the national labor organizations. In the United States, these unions can not engage in collective bargaining with the government, though they exert influence through lobbying and public opinion to secure salary increases and other benefits. In Britain, the Whitley Councils and in France, the "representative commissions," both established for settlement of grievances, amount to agencies for collective bargaining. In the United States and Britain, strikes against the government are forbidden, but in France and Italy, such strikes have occurred, usually to exert political pressure. In these countries, civil servants are not forbidden to take active part in politics. In the Soviet Union, where all economic enterprise is operated by the government, all workers are government employees. They all *must* belong to labor unions, but these unions have no rights of collective bargaining and are forbidden to strike. Administrators, from the lowest to the highest, are seleced on the basis of party status and favoritism, and make up a real bureaucracy.

INDIVIDUAL COUNTRIES — THE UNITED STATES. The administration of the national civil service in the United States is directed by the Civil Service Commission, a bi-partisan group of three members created by Congress. Congress makes and changes the general rules by legislation, but the Commission, with the approval of the President, makes and enforces the detailed rules. Our foreign service has its own similar but separate system administered by a bureau in the Department of State. Each individual state has its own arrangements, many of them still filling most jobs under the old spoils‧system. The competitive examinations are "practical," in that they are based on qualifications for a particular job or type of work, rather than on general education. We did not start out with the idea that the civil service is a life career, but this viewpoint is making steady headway. The examinations are open to any citizen, not tainted with disloyalty, who has whatever training or education may be needed for the particular job or type of work. We do not, like most countries, divide the civil service into definite ranks, each geared to a certain level of general education, but the educational prerequisites for some of the higher positions may include high school, or even college. Those who pass the examination with a minimum grade, are rated on an eligibility list in the order of their examination grade as altered by allowing extra credit to veterans and veterans' widows, and in some cases, extra credit for prior experience in similar work.

Appointments are then made under the "rule of three." When a vacancy occurs, the three highest names on the list are submitted to the appointing officer, who usually interviews the persons named. He then selects one of the three, and the other two go back on the list. This rule is not followed in any other country. It is made necessary in our case by the constitutional provision that Congress may vest the appointment of inferior officers in the President alone, the courts of law, or the heads of departments. The eligibility list may be narrowed (to no less than three, it has been decided) but, unless the appointing officer is left some freedom of choice, the whole scheme would be unconstitutional.

There are promotions in the ranks, of course, but they rarely go as high as the top positions in the service. Nor does the service itself extend as high in government as in many countries. The attitude of regarding the civil service as a life career is making steady headway, but such a career still does not carry the social prestige that it does in Britain, France or West Germany.

GREAT BRITAIN. The British merit system differs from the American in several important respects. When it was adopted more than a century ago, copying a scheme the East India Company had worked out for the civil service of India, the British civil service was already regarded as a career with social prestige, but it was recruited on a basis of favoritism from younger sons of lords or other wealthy persons, and was grossly inefficient. Concerned with attracting people with greater ability and devotion to the service, the British geared their system to general education and divided the service into four ranks based on the education required. At the bottom, are the *clerical* and *subclerical* ranks, open to anyone with an elementary school education through "practical" entrance examinations. People in these ranks do routine work, and only the most capable win promotion to the next higher rank. Above these comes the *executive* rank, limited to secondary school graduates, and at the top the *administrative* rank, limited to university graduates. Entrance examinations for these higher ranks are of the "comprehensive" type, based on the curricula of the schools attended. People who go into these ranks are entering a life career, rather than getting a job, so that general education is considered more important than the knowledge required for a particular position. Those in the top rank may rise as high as permanent secretaries of departments, who manage all of the departmental administration and often influence the decisions of the political department heads. When a permanent secretary retires he is given at least the rank of knighthood, and sometimes a peerage.

Appointments are made partly on the basis of examination grades, partly on interviews. Promotions are based mainly on service records. Britain does not maintain special training schools for its civil servants, but does provide in-service training through scholarships to universities.

FRANCE. In many ways, the French civil service resembles the British. It, too, is geared to general education, and is divided into the same four ranks. It is distinctive in maintaining a special training school, the National School of Administration, to prepare civil servants for the higher administrative positions. Examinations to enter this school may be taken by graduates of universities or special schools of university level, and also by civil servants with five years experience in lower administrative positions. In the past, political ministers sometimes infiltrated their followers into the civil service, but this practice has ceased under the Fifth Republic.

WEST GERMANY. The West German civil service is much more bureaucratic than these others because its upper ranks are largely monopolized by a self-perpetuating official class that goes back to the old Kingdom of Prussia. There are entrance examinations geared to the different levels of education as in Britain and France. There is even sharper division than in Britain and France between the upper and lower ranks. Entrance into the upper ranks is limited to graduates of certain schools who are also trained in law. There is little turnover, and promotion is slow. Most of the new recruits are sons of older civil servants. They are not forbidden to take part in politics, but they take little interest. They do, however, exert greater influence on government policy making than do the civil servants of most other countries.

ITALY. The civil service of Italy is still "unreformed." There have been gestures of introducing a merit system, but almost no progress has been made. Appointments are still made on the basis of politics. The service is notorious for its inefficiency, and corruption turns up all too frequently.

Administrative Law

WHAT IS ADMINISTRATIVE LAW? The enormous growth in the extent and volume of administrative work has produced, in most countries, a body of law dealing with administrative matters. This administrative law falls into three broad categories. First, there are laws creating and regulating the administrative agencies. Some of these may be embodied in the constitution, and some may be "decree laws" issued by the executive. Most of them, though, are statutes enacted by the legislative body. In general, these laws may be tested, interpreted and enforced in the regular courts. Second, there are laws made by administrative bodies, and finally there are laws to provide redress for persons who claim to have been injured improperly by the administrative processes.

QUASI-LEGISLATIVE AND QUASI-JUDICIAL POWERS. Some administrative agencies, especially those with regulatory or managerial functions, can make law of an inferior grade in either or both of two ways. Quasi-legislative or rule making power is the power to issue regulations that have the force of law, but which may be overruled by statutes. The quasi-judicial power is the power to make decisions that resemble court decisions and are binding unless they are overruled by a court. Both of these types of administrative law making are subject to judicial review. That is, a party who is affected adversely may appeal the regulation or the order for enforcing the decision to a court, which will pass on the validity of the administrative action. In common law countries (Great Britain, the United States, Canada, Australia and New Zealand) this judicial review is always by regular courts. In other countries, it may be partly by regular courts and partly by special administrative courts.

REDRESS FOR TORTS. A tort is an injury which is not punishable as a crime, but for which the injured party may sue for damages. It is a rule of both common law and Roman law that the citizen can not sue the government without its consent. This would seem to leave the private individual (or business firm) without redress if he suffers damage from the negligence or other fault of agents of the government in their official acts. However, the American Congress has passed a Tort Claims Act which permits a private party to sue the government on torts. These suits are in regular courts and are handled according to the same rules that would apply in damage suits against another private party. In Britain, numerous administrative commissions have been set up to judge such cases, with appeals to the regular courts.

In several countries of continental Europe, special administrative courts, separate from the regular courts and with no appeal to them, have been set up to handle such cases. In France, there are twenty-four regional administrative courts, each consisting of a judge and four councillors. They handle not only tort claims, but also complaints about administrative orders and regulations. Appeals may be taken to the Council of State, which serves both as the highest administrative court, and as an advisory body to the executive and parliament. Italy and Germany also have systems of administrative courts, but they handle only complaints about administrative orders and regulations. In both of these countries, tort claims are handled in the regular courts, much as in the United States.

Initially these administrative courts had little positive law to guide them. There were a few executive decrees and a few statutory provisions, but no general code of administrative law which they could apply. Consequently, each case had to be decided on its own merits as evaluated by the judges. Like other courts, though, administrative courts tend to follow precedent. Once a case involving certain issues has been decided, subsequent cases involving the same issues are usually decided the same way. Thus, in much the same manner in which the Roman law and the common law developed originally, these courts have built up a body of rules which they follow. In France, these rules are being consolidated into a definite code.

Local Administration

NATIONAL AND LOCAL. Much of the work of national administration is carried on at a local level through regional branches or local offices of national agencies, such as, in our country, local weather stations and post offices, and regional federal revenue offices and social security offices. There are other matters, though, that are strictly local in character and are administered by agencies of counties, cities, or other subdivisions. Detailed discussion of this local administration must await our chapter on local government, but a few points may be in order here.

LOCAL AGENCIES. Direction of a particular area of local administration may be under the direction of a single official or of a collective group, a board or commission. These may be either elective or appointive. In most democratic countries, there is a locally elected council or board which has general oversight of administration in its area. In the United States, we usually elect a large number of county administrative officers. In most countries, these officers, or the boards, commissions or committees that replace them, are selected by the local council. In unitary states, these local agencies owe their existence to the national government, and are responsible to it for the conduct of their work. In federal unions, they are creatures of the component unit (state, *Land*, province, etc.) and are similarly responsible to its government.

CENTRALIZATION OF CONTROL. Except insofar as their status and powers are defined in the constitution, these local agencies are always subject to control by legislation of the government, national or state, to which they are responsible. They may also be subject to some administrative control. In the United States, federal administrative control is limited to conditions imposed in the grants-in-aid made for such projects as public housing, urban renewal and welfare projects. In some cases, the governor of the state appoints local boards to administer elections, police, and possibly other matters. In West Germany, the federal government may assume authority, in emergency situations, over state (*Land*) and local administration, but so far it has not done so. In Britain, the ministries control some local boards and commissions, but have no authority over the borough and county councils or their committees which act as administrative agencies. In France and Italy, a representative of the Ministry of the Interior, the prefect (under the Fifth Republic in France his title has been changed to "delegate of the government") has what amounts to veto power on acts of the *department* or provincial council, particularly when national interests are involved. Several smaller countries of Europe also have officials corresponding to the prefect. In the Soviet Union, all actions of local councils are checked by a representative of the Communist Party and by a member of the political police.

Suggested Questions for Discussion

1. What is the difference in meaning between "administration" and "the administration"? Why is administration so important in modern government?

2. Through what type of agencies is administration carried on? For what purposes is each type best suited?

3. Compare the varying degrees of centralized and decentralized administration found in: (1) the United States, (2) Great Britain, (3) France, (4) Italy and (5) West Germany.

4. What is meant by "civil service"? What are the various meanings of "bureaucracy"? At what point does bureaucracy become detrimental?

5. Why have most countries adopted some kind of merit system for their administrative employees? Compare major features of the merit systems of: (1) the United States, (2) Great Britain, (3) France and (4) West Germany.

6. See how complete a list you can make of administrative functions.

7. What are "quasi-legislative" and "quasi-judicial" powers? Why do some administrative agencies have these powers?

8. What is administrative law? How and why has it developed? How is it administered in different countries?

9. Compare the roles of elective boards or their committees in supervising local administration in the major countries.

10. To what extent and in what manner are local administrative officials supervised by national or state governments in various countries?
11. Only in the United States are large numbers of local administrative officials popularly elected. What are the arguments for and against the plan?
12. What are the rules in various countries about suing the government on tort claims?

Bibliography

Dawson, R. G., The Civil Service in Canada (New York, 1939)

Gladden, E. N., The Essentials of Public Administration (New York, 1955)

Morstein-Marx, F., Elements of Public Administration (Englewood Cliffs, N. J., 1959)

Sharp, W. R., The French Civil Service: Bureaucracy in Transition (New York, 1931)

Sisson, C. H., Spirit of British Administration (New York, 1959)

SEVEN

Law and Courts

Nature and Sources of Law

MEANING OF LAW. Law, in what is called the juridical sense, means the body of rules, enforceable in the courts, which regulate the conduct and relations of individuals. It may or may not be systematized into a code, which is a classification and statement of the rules of law. One branch, called criminal law, defines crimes and prescribes their punishment. The other branch, called civil law in English speaking countries,* regulates the relationship of individuals in property holding, business, domestic relations, and other activities, and provides redress for those who suffer injuries. It is sometimes said that law is whatever the courts will enforce.

SOURCES OF LAW. We usually think of law as having been enacted by a legislative body. Much of it is. Some of it may be in the form of executive orders or decrees, and some of it may be made by administrative bodies with quasi-legislative power. In some cases, the courts will enforce long-standing customs or traditions as law. A great deal of the law, as actually applied, is judge-made law. Confronted with a case for which there are no exact precedents, the judges will make a rule to fit the case, either by reinterpreting an old rule (statutory or otherwise) or by applying what they consider principles of justice. Both of our great legal systems, the Roman law and the common law of England, were developed in this way.

* As we shall see presently, the term civil law also has another meaning as the name of the Roman system of law.

Major Systems of Law

SYSTEMS OF LAW. Aside from a few countries of Asia and Africa that have very unsystematic bodies of law that are rooted deeply in their remote past, there are four major systems of law in the world. These are the English common law, the Roman civil law, Moslem law, and the "Marxism-Leninism," of Communist countries. By a system of law we mean a body of rules and principles that provide the basis for the legislation and the judge-made law in countries that follow the particular system. Included in these rules and principles are some basic features of court procedure that characterize one system as distinct from others.

THE COMMON LAW. As already indicated, the common law grew up through decisions of royal courts during the later centuries of the Middle Ages. By the beginning of modern times, it had crystallized into a body of rules that covered just about every legal issue that could arise in court as well as a number of basic principles of jurisprudence. Among its distinctive features are trial by jury, due process of law, habeas corpus, and other procedural rights to guarantee to litigants a fair and impartial trial. It deals mainly with matters involved in civil suits, where one private party sues another, but it also recognizes certain common law crimes. Today it is the basis of the legal systems of Great Britain and all countries that have developed out of British colonies, including the United States. It is also followed with modifications in all countries that were formerly dependencies of either Britain or the United States. Many of the old rules have been modified by statute; in some of our American states, most of them have been enacted into statutes with little or no change. The old common law principles still apply, though, and when a point comes up that is not covered by a statute, the judges still fall back on an old rule of common law.

ROMAN CIVIL LAW. Roman law, or the civil law as it is often called, developed in much the same manner during the first five centuries of the Christian era. It was codified under the direction of the Emperor Justinian in the sixth century. In the Middle Ages, it was the basis of much of the canon law that was applied in Church courts. In early modern times, all the countries of continental Western Europe used the Roman law, but much of it did not fit modern conditions. To remedy this, Napoleon Bonaparte, at the beginning of the 19th century, had the Roman law adapted and codified in what is still known as the Code Napoleon. In this form, Roman or civil law is today the basis of the legal systems of all continental European countries west of the iron curtain, and of countries in other parts of the world that have grown out of French, Spanish or Portuguese colonies. Many of the rules of civil law are similar to rules of common law, but many are very different. Its principles of jurisprudence are entirely different, lacking the procedural safeguards for the rights of litigants and allowing the judge a much wider range of discretion.

MOSLEM LAW. In most Moslem countries, the Koran is the basis of the legal system. The sayings of Mohammed, as recorded in the Koran, are considered sacrosanct rules of law. The most that a ruler or a legislative body can do is to interpret these sayings and spell out their application in particular situations. In modern times, in these countries, there are legislation and judge-made law on subjects not touched upon in the Koran, but these follow Moslem principles, much as, in the English speaking countries, they follow the principles of common law. Court procedure is largely arbitrary, with the judge deciding everything. Protection of the rights of litigants and accused persons is less adequate under Roman law than under common law, but under Moslem law such protection is non-existent.

MARXISM-LENINISM. In the Soviet Union and other Communist countries, law is what the party oligarchy decides it is. It is subject to change at any time, not only by formal legislation, but by directives handed down from party headquarters to the judges. The courts exist less to administer justice than to enforce the party line. There are few civil cases in the courts since, with the government owning and operating all economic activities and arbitrarily controlling all social relationships, there is not much about which one private party can sue another. In criminal prosecutions, the accused has little chance to defend himself, and the procedure centers around efforts to extort confessions, regardless of factual guilt or innocence. In spite of this, Soviet courts are lenient (perhaps too lenient) in dealing with offenses against individuals, but are merciless in punishing offenses against the state.

Court Systems and Judicial Procedure

COURTS AND THEIR JURISDICTION. A court is a judge, or group of judges acting jointly, which adjudicates disputes (that is, decides them by a judicial process) between private parties or between a private party and the government; it may also try persons accused of criminal offenses. Jurisdiction means the authority of a court. The term is also used to mean the classes or types of cases over which a court, or set of courts, has authority. A court in which cases are brought and tried has original jurisdiction; it is called a court of first instance because it gets cases first, before they are carried to higher courts on appeal. A court which receives cases on appeal from lower courts has appellate jurisdiction. If its main business is hearing cases on appeal, it is called an appellate court, even though it may have original jurisdiction in some cases. In the United States, with a few minor exceptions, the same courts handle both criminal prosecutions and civil cases. Some countries have separate courts for these types of cases.

COURT SYSTEMS. Each country has its own system of courts and no two are exactly alike. The courts of a country form a pyramid, or perhaps two parallel pyramids, one for civil and one for criminal cases. At the base of the pyramid are a large number of petty courts, each with jurisdiction over a very small geographical area, for the settlement of small disputes and the trial of minor offenses. These are usually presided over by non-professional judges, such as justices of the peace or the *juges de paix* in France. Cities usually have their own petty courts for strictly municipal matters. At a slightly higher level, and with jurisdiction over a larger area, such as the British or American county, are the principal courts of first instance. Most cases come to these courts for their original trial, along with appeals from the petty courts. Above these, there are a smaller number of appeal courts, and at the apex of the pyramid, the supreme court, or court of cassation as it is called in some countries. We can not, of course, look into the court system of every country, but we may glance briefly at a few of the most important.

THE UNITED STATES. In federal unions, each component unit has its own court system, with some variation from unit to unit. There may or may not be a parallel system of federal courts, starting with courts of first instance. In some federal unions, the only federal court with general jurisdiction is a federal supreme court, though there may be one or more special federal courts, such as a constitutional court and a federal administrative court, which do not handle ordinary litigation. In these countries, federal cases, up to a possible final appeal to the federal supreme court, are handled by the courts of the component units. Our Constitutional Convention of 1787 discussed such an arrangement for the United States, but left the decision to Congress by providing that "The judicial power of the United States shall be vested in one Supreme Court, and in such inferior courts as the Congress may from time to time ordain and establish." The first Congress, however, decided upon a separate system of federal courts, and we have had such a system ever since.

The court system in the individual American state follows, with variations, the standard pyramidal pattern. At the lowest level are justice of the peace, magistrate or police courts, usually several to a county, for the trial of petty cases. At the county level is the circuit or district court which is the principal court of first instance. The state usually has two or more intermediate courts of appeals, each serving a designated portion of the state. At the top of the pyramid is the state supreme court. The federal system begins with United States district Courts, at least one to each state. These are the courts of first instance for most federal cases. They are one-judge courts. If a district has more than one judge, each holds court separately and only for a few special purposes do they act jointly as a panel. There are ten United States Courts of Appeals, each with five or more judges. At the top is the Supreme Court of the United States with nine justices.

In the United States, federal and state jurisdictions are sharply defined. The Constitution of the United States lists the classes of cases in which the federal courts have jurisdiction, and all other cases must begin and end in state courts. A case may be transferred or appealed from state to federal courts only if it involves a federal question; that is, if it comes under one of the classes of cases over which the federal courts have jurisdiction.

There are also some special federal courts. There is a court of claims, legally a part of the regular court system, which adjudicates all claims against the government except tort claims, which are handled by the district courts. Classed as "legislative" courts, because they do not come under the constitutional jurisdiction, are a customs court, which decides disputes about customs charges, and a Court of Customs and Patent Appeals, which hears appeals from this court and from the Patent Office. In many countries, these would be classed as administrative courts. There are also federal courts, likewise classed as legislative, for the territories, dependencies and the District of Columbia.

In United States federal courts, all judges are appointed for life terms by the President, with the confirmation of the Senate, and may be removed only by impeachment. There are no qualifications but, in practice, the persons appointed are almost always trained lawyers. Promotions from a district court to a court of appeals are not unusual, but promotions from a court of appeals to the Supreme Court are rare. Supreme Court justices, though always lawyers, are more apt to have a background in politics than on the bench. The states vary in their practices, but in most of them judges are elected for fixed terms. Some states do and some do not have a requirement that judges be lawyers.

GREAT BRITAIN. The court system we are sketching here should be referred to as English rather than British. Since

1703, Scotland has been united with England and Wales for most government purposes, but it retains its separate system of law (similar to the English common law, but differing in details) and its separate courts. The English court system evolved during the later Middle Ages and, despite increasing conflicts of jurisdiction, it remained unchanged until the Judicature Act of 1873. Besides justices of the peace for petty cases, and several courts at the county level, there were three principal national courts, with original jurisdiction in important cases, which also heard appeals from the courts in the counties. These were the Court of King's Bench for criminal cases, the Court of Common Pleas for civil cases, and the Court of Chancery for equity cases. There was also a Court of Exchequer, something like our Court of Claims and Customs Court, which handled financial claims against the government, chiefly appeals from tax assessments.

Beginning in 1873, Parliament passed a series of Judicature Acts which undertook to systematize the court structure with separate courts (but not always separate judges) for civil and criminal cases. On the civil side, there is a county court in each county, with one county judge, for small civil suits. Appeals go directly from the county court to the Court of Appeal. In London, there is what is called the Supreme Court of Judicature, which combines the functions of the historic high courts, but is a single court in name only. It is divided into two levels, the High Court of Justice and the Court of Appeal. The High Court, which now has original jurisdiction only, consists of three divisions: King's Bench (Queen's Bench, when the country has a Queen instead of a King), with the Lord Chief Justice and nineteen judges, for ordinary civil cases; Chancery, with the Lord Chancellor and five judges, for equity cases, including bankruptcy; Probate, Divorce and Admiralty, with a President and seven judges, whose functions are indicated by the title. Each division operates separately. The Court of Appeal consists of the Master of Rolls and eight Lord Justices. It takes appeals from the county courts and also from the divisions of the High Court. A few very important cases may be appealed from the Court of Appeal to the House of Lords.

On the criminal side, there is a justice of the peace in every rural locality, and in every town larger than a rural village, one or more stipendiary magistrates. These differ from justices of the peace chiefly in that they receive a salary; justices of the peace are paid only in fees they collect. The justice of the peace or magistrate may try and punish very minor offenses without a jury. Two or more justices of the peace may act jointly as a court of petty sessions to try without jury persons accused of slightly more serious offenses, and to hold preliminary hearings of persons accused of serious crimes to determine whether there is enough evidence to justify sending them to a higher court for jury trial. All the justices of the peace in a county meet, traditionally four times a year, as the court of quarter sessions. They try, with jury, offenses that do not require specialized judicial knowledge. In each county there is also a Court of Assize, formerly called a circuit court. It is presided over by a judge of the King's Bench Division of the High Court, and is the court of original jurisdiction for major crimes. Each King's Bench judge, except the three who serve on the Court of Criminal Appeal, in addition to his duties in London, has a circuit of several counties (hence the term circuit court) and must visit each one for as long as necessary each year to hold Assize Court. Appeals may be taken by defendants convicted in either Quarter Sessions or Assize Court to the Court of Criminal Appeal in London. It consists of three judges of the King's Bench Division of the High Court. Unlike the typical appellate court, this court retries cases. In extremely rare instances, appeals may be allowed from the Court of Criminal Appeal to the House of Lords.

The House of Lords is the highest court of appeal in both civil and criminal cases, but it accepts only cases involving the clarification of some very important point of law. When acting as a court, the House of Lords consists of the Lord Chancellor, who is always a trained jurist, and nine Lords of Appeal in Ordinary, commonly called the law lords. They are jurists of long experience who are appointed peers for life especially for this work. Except for ceremonies, they take no part in other activities of the House of Lords. Other peers who are experienced jurists may take part in judicial proceedings of the Lords, but rarely do. There is also a court, miscalled the Judicial Committee of the Privy Council, which is a supreme court for colonial and Commonwealth affairs. Some Commonwealth countries permit appeal of cases to the Judicial Committee, and some do not. In theory, the Judicial Committee is still what it evolved from, a committee of the Privy Council to recommend summary action to the monarch. In reality, it has become a true court. It is presided over by the Lord President of the Council, a cabinet member, but its judges are the same nine law lords who act for the House of Lords.

In the English system, there are no elective judges. All are appointed for life by the Crown, on recommendation of the Lord Chancellor. All above the rank of justice of the peace or stipendiary magistrate, are trained lawyers.

FRANCE. The French court structure resembles the English in many respects, but is more systematic. In each commune (the smallest political subdivision) there is at least one justice of the peace court (in France, justices of the peace are called *juges de paix,* judges of the land). Besides deciding very small civil disputes and punishing very minor offenses, the justice of the peace acts as a conciliator to try to settle civil disputes out of court. In the larger communes there are also industrial disputes councils, made up of representatives of workers and employers, to adjust local labor disputes, and commercial tribunals, made up of representative local businessmen, to settle arguments over business transactions. These are classed as conciliation courts. The country is divided into more than three hundred districts, each of which has a court of first instance. This court has two sections, each with three judges, one for civil and one for criminal cases. The civil section has original jurisdiction in almost all civil cases, and hears appeals from the justices of the peace and the industrial disputes councils. The criminal section takes appeals from the justices of the peace and has original jurisdiction in trials for crimes of medium seriousness. It does not use a jury. Above the courts of first instances, on the civil side, are twenty-seven appeal courts, each with five judges (except in Paris, where there are seven). It takes cases appealed from the civil sections of the courts of first instance and the commercial tribunals, retries them, and gives the final verdict on facts. Appeals from this court can be taken only on points of law. Of equal rank with the appeal courts, on the criminal side, are the assize courts, one for each *department*. Each assize court has a judge of an appeal court as president, and three judges who are also judges of a court of first instance. It has original jurisdiction in trials of major crimes, which are tried by a jury, and hears appeals from the criminal section of courts of first instance, which it settles without a jury.

At the top of the pyramid is the Court of Cassation or supreme court. It has three distinct sections, each with sixteen judges: petitions, civil and criminal. The petitions section passes on petitions for equity remedies. The civil and criminal sections take appeals from the appeal courts and assize courts respectively, but only on points of law. There are two other courts at the national level; the Council of State as supreme administrative court, and the Constitutional Court which only rules on questions of constitutionality or constitutional interpretation at the request of the President of the Republic or other national official.

Unlike English and American judges, French judges, along with public prosecutors, form a distinct profession and are virtually a branch of the civil service. After getting his law degree, the prospective "magistrate" serves a term of apprenticeship, either as an assistant to a judge or as an assistant prosecutor, and then takes a competitive qualifying examination. When his turn comes, on the basis of his examination grade, he is appointed to a minor judgeship. He is promoted from time to time, his promotion often involving a transfer to another part of the country. Not all can reach the top, of course, but judges of the Court of Cassation come up through this line of promotion. Appointments are made by the President of the Republic on recommendation of the High Council of the Judiciary. This is a partly *ex officio,* partly appointive body, which also has disciplinary authority over judges and advises the President of the Republic on pardons.

ITALY. The Italian judicial structure was copied largely from the French and resembles it very closely. At the base of the pyramid are petty judges, called conciliators, similar to justices of the peace. Like their French counterparts, they are paid only in fees and are not professional judges. The lowest regular judge is the·praetor, at least one to each province, who has original jurisdiction in minor civil and criminal cases. At the next level, one to each province, are a tribunal for civil cases and an assize court for criminal cases. Each consists of a panel of at least three judges, and has original jurisdiction in major cases; it also hears appeals from the court of the praetor. Above these, for a region or special district, are twin appellate courts: a Court of Appeal of five judges to review decisions of the tribunals in civil cases, and an Assize Appellate Court, with two judges and five lay "assessors," who are experts in various fields, to act on appeals from the assize courts. At the top is the Supreme Court of Cassation which, besides deciding jurisdictional questions, takes appeals from the appellate courts on questions of law only. There is a Supreme Council of the Judiciary which closely resembles the French "High Council" and has the same functions. Also as in France, there is a Council of State, which is the supreme administrative court, and a Constitutional Court with the same functions as the Constitutional Court in France.

Italian judges, like the French, are professionals, and a part of the civil service. Their recruitment and promotion follow the same lines. Judicial appointments are made by the President of Italy on recommendation of the Supreme Council of the Judiciary.

WEST GERMANY. As in Switzerland, Australia and the Soviet Union, the only federal court for general litigation is the Federal Supreme Court. As in France and Italy, there is also a constitutional court and a supreme administrative court, but these are not considered a part of the regular court system. The Supreme Court has three sections, each with five judges: a civil section, a criminal section for appeals, and a criminal section with original jurisdiction. Except for the trial of a few serious federal crimes, which go directly to the third section of the Supreme Court, cases under federal law, both civil and criminal, originate and have their first appeal in the courts of

the *Länder* (states). However, since the court system goes
back, with little change, to the old German Empire of 1871-
1918, the systems in the *Länder* are remarkably uniform.
There is nothing corresponding to justices of the peace. The
lowest court (we usually translate its German name simply
"local court") is a one judge court in each township, which
corresponds to the court of the praetor in Italy. It has both
civil and criminal jurisdiction in minor cases. In all but the
most trivial criminal cases, the judge is assisted by two lay
assessors. The *Land* is divided into a number of judicial districts, each with a district court of several sections. A civil
appeal section with three judges hears appeals in civil suits
from the local court. Another civil section, also with three
judges, has original jurisdiction in more important civil cases.
There are three criminal sections. One called "the little chamber," with one judge and two lay assessors, takes appeals in
misdemeanor cases from the local court. Another, called the
"big chamber," with three judges and two lay assessors, hears
appeals in cases of more serious offenses from the local court,
and has original jurisdiction in the trial of most major crimes.
Another section, called assize court, has original jurisdiction
in the trial of the most serious crimes. Appeals in all major
criminal cases go directly from the district court to the criminal appeal section of the Federal Supreme Court. For the appeal of all other cases, each *Land* has a court of appeal, the
highest court at the state level. It has a civil section and a
criminal section, with three judges each, for appeals from the
local courts. Civil cases may be appealed from its decisions
to the civil section of the Federal Supreme Court.

German judges, like French and Italian, form a profession
apart. The young man who wants a career in "the administration of justice," first receives special training in a university.
Then, if he can pass a qualifying examination, he has a period of in-service training in a court or prosecutor's office.
Then, if he can pass a rigid second examination, he is ready
for appointment to a minor judgeship or as an assistant prosecutor. From then on, it is a matter of winning promotions.
Appointments in the *Land* courts are made by the *Land* minister of justice, but the real selections are made by the older

and more influential judges. Members of the Federal Supreme Court are selected by a special commission, and are appointed formally by the President of the Federal Republic.

THE SOVIET UNION. Although nominally a federal union, the U.S.S.R. has a single unified system of courts. In every locality or factory, there is a "comradly court" to settle minor disputes between individuals. At a slightly higher level is a "people's court," with one judge and two lay assessors, with original jurisdiction in minor civil and criminal cases. In both these courts, the judges are elected for three-year terms by local citizens. For each region there is a regional court of five judges, with original jurisdiction in more important civil and criminal cases, except crimes against the state, and appellate jurisdiction in cases coming up from lower courts. For each of the fifteen member republics, there is a union-republic supreme court of five judges. It has original jurisdiction in crimes against the state, and appellate jurisdiction in all other cases. Judges of these two courts are elected for five year terms by the soviet of their area. Finally, there is the All-Union Supreme Court with twelve judges elected for five year terms by the Supreme Soviet. It is divided into civil, criminal and military sections. Though mainly an appellate court, it has original jurisdiction in the trial of high public officials and military officers. At each level up to the "all-union," there is a public prosecutor, appointed for a five year term by the All-Union Procurator General, who in turn is elected for a seven year term by the Supreme Soviet. Although all judges and prosecutors are elective, the real choices are by a Communist Party committee at the level involved.

COURT PROCEDURE. In common law countries, trial courts are usually one judge courts; appellate courts are always panels of three or more judges. These appellate courts never retry a case; they only review it on points of law and procedure. If a retrial is in order, the case is sent back to a trial court. In most other countries, only the lowest court is a one judge court; all others are panels, regardless of their type of jurisdiction.

Procedure in common law countries is based on the princi-

ple that every litigant, and especially defendants in criminal
prosecutions above the petty level, is entitled to "due process
of law." This means that he must be given every opportunity
to defend himself and what he considers to be his rights. In
criminal prosecutions (except for minor "police" cases) this
involves the right of trial by jury. Juries are also used in civil
cases involving large sums of money, if either party demands
it, and in tort cases to determine the amount of damages to
be awarded. France has taken over the jury for the trial of
some major offenses. In other countries, the functions of a jury
are performed in part by lay assessors. These are persons who
are not lawyers though, in some countries, such as France and
Italy, they are usually experts in some matter involved in the
trial. Unlike jurors, who hear the evidence and give a verdict,
but can not participate in the trial otherwise, these lay assessors may question witnesses, give evidence themselves, and
advise the judge at any point in the trial.

Most free countries try to keep their courts as independent
of political influence as possible, but in totalitarian lands the
courts are an instrument of state policy. Ideas of even-handed
justice are never allowed to stand in the way of enforcing the
will of the ruling party oligarchy. Partly for this reason, perhaps, Soviet court procedure borders on the chaotic. Prosecutions of crimes against the state, with their shouted denuncia-
tions and their extorted confessions, are more like a public
spectacle than a dignified trial at law.

Judicial Guardianship of Constitutions

JUDICIAL REVIEW OF LEGISLATION. In the United States,
we think of guardianship of the Constitution by the courts,
especially by the Supreme Court, as a vitally important judicial function. In the form in which we know it, called judicial
review of legislation, it is distinctively American. It originated
in colonial times when an aggrieved party could appeal a case
from the highest court in the colony to the Judicial Committee
of the Privy Council in England, alleging that the colonial
statute which was the basis for the decision in the colonial
courts was in violation either of the colonial charter or the

constitutional laws of England. If the Judicial Committee agreed with the allegation, it would, in the King's name, "disallow" or nullify the statute. The first annulment of a law by an American court, claiming the former jurisdiction of the Judicial Committee, was in the famous "Know Ye" case in Rhode Island in 1787, the year of the Constitutional Convention. The delegates to that convention considered a proposal to grant this power to the United States Supreme Court, but failed to agree and left the question open. Very soon, however, in the case of Marbury vs. Madison in 1803, the Supreme Court assumed the power. Only a few other countries, mostly in Latin America, have copied the arrangement from us.

Any American court can pass on the constitutionality of a law, either state or federal, but the last word lies with the Supreme Court of the United States. A court will rule on constitutionality only in the process of deciding a case before it. Unlike some of the constitutional courts of Europe, our Supreme Court will not advise the executive or the legislative branch on the constitutionality of a proposed law in advance of enactment. Neither will it rule abstractly on the question after the law is enacted. Only when the constitutionality of the law is challenged by a litigant in a regular law suit, will an American court pass judgment on the issue. In doing so, our courts not only safeguard the Constitution, but they also interpret it, and this judicial interpretation has done much to give our Constitution the flexibility it has needed to adjust to changing conditions with comparatively little formal amendment.

In many countries, England and the Soviet Union among them, there is no judicial guardianship of the constitution at all. In Switzerland, the Federal Tribunal, as they call their supreme court, will not pass on the constitutionality of acts of the Swiss parliament, but it does apply judicial review in cases coming up from the courts of the cantons to determine if a cantonal law violates the federal constitution.

CONSTITUTIONAL COURTS. As already noted, several European countries, including France, Italy and West Germany, have set up constitutional courts. These do not operate on the basis of judicial review. Rather, on application of the proper official, they will advise the executive or the parliament on the constitutionality of a proposed law in advance of its enactment. They usually have other functions also, such as interpreting constitutional provisions and ruling on the status of various types of legislative enactments. They do, in their own way, though, safeguard the constitution against violations by other branches of government.

Suggested Questions for Discussion

1. Explain the meaning of: (1) law; (2) courts; (3) legal systems.
2. Describe the various ways in which laws come into existence. What is "judge-made law"?
3. What are the major systems of law in the modern world? Where is each used? What are some of the distinctive features of each?
4. Compare the court systems of: (1) the United States, (2) Great Britain, (3) France, (4) West Germany, (5) Italy and (6) the Soviet Union.
5. Contrast distinctive features of court procedure under common law and the Code Napoleon.
6. Compare the relative merits of juries and "lay assessors" in court procedure.
7. In what countries are administrative courts found? Describe their structure and functions. How is their place taken in other countries?
8. How is the British House of Lords different when sitting as a court and when sitting as a legislative body?
9. What major countries have judicial guardianship of the constitution? How and to what extent is the constitution safeguarded in other countries?
10. What countries have constitutional courts? Compare the way they function in the different countries.
11. Compare the good and bad features of constitutional courts and American "judicial review" as methods of safeguarding the constitution.
12. Compare the methods of selecting judges in the various countries (and in the component units of federal unions). What is to be said for and against each method?

Bibliography

Daiches, L., Russians at Law (Toronto, 1960)

Duhamel, J., and Smith, J. D., Some Pillars of English Law (Toronto, 1959)

Ensor, R., Courts and Judges in France, Germany and England (New York, 1933)

Hanburg, H. G., English Courts of Law (New York, 1953)

Schwartz, B., Ed., The Code Napoleon and the Common Law World (New York, 1956)

Wagner, W. J., Federal States and Their Judiciary (New York, 1959)

EIGHT

Local Government

Scope of Local Government

WHAT ARE LOCAL GOVERNMENTS? Thus far we have been discussing national governments and the governments of component units of federal unions, each of which possesses sovereign powers. These governments do touch the individual citizen directly through taxation, regulatory laws, and nationalized services. They can not, however, handle directly a great many matters that touch the life of the people at the everyday level. To deal with these matters, the national state or the component unit in a federal system is divided into territorial subdivisions, known by different names in different countries, each of which has governmental functions. There are always at least two, and sometimes more, levels of such subdivisions. These may be primarily administrative units, but usually they have some limited power of local self government. In some countries, but not all, cities have a separate status from the territorial subdivision in which they are located, and usually enjoy a large measure of self government.

CREATURES OF A SOVEREIGN STATE. Legally, these local government units are creatures of the sovereign state in which they are located. Provision may be made for them in the constitution of such state, or they may be set up by ordinary law. Cities, especially in the common law countries, may have charters which give them their legal existence and confer their powers upon them. In any case, the local units are subject to the laws of the state and the decisions of its courts, and are under greater or less degree of administrative control. They usually have some financial powers of their own, conferred by law or by their charter, but these are exercised subject to state control. If they have legislative power, their laws or ordinances must not conflict with the laws of the state.

FEDERAL AND UNITARY STATES. We have had numerous occasions to note the distinction between federal and unitary states. In unitary states, such as Great Britain and France, where there is only one level of government with sovereign powers, the governmental subdivisions are divisions of the country as a whole, and are subject directly to the authority of the central government. In federal unions, like the United States and Canada, they are divisions of the component unit, the "state" or province, and are subject to its authority and its laws. In quasi-federal states like West Germany, they are divisions of the component unit (the *Land* in Germany) but in some instances the central government may exercise authority over them.

FUNCTIONS OF LOCAL GOVERNMENT. Whether or not they possess any real local self government, what we call local government units are always administrative divisions or subdivisions of the state to perform certain state functions at a local level. They usually assess and collect the property taxes and sometimes other state taxes as well. They keep the records of real estate transactions and such vital statistics as births, marriages and deaths. They are local units for the conducting of elections and are usually the area of operation of one or more of the state courts. In many countries, they maintain and operate the public schools, and they may have some freedom of action in building local roads and in maintaining such local institutions as hospitals, social service institutions and recreational facilities. Cities, and sometimes other local units, may have limited power to make and enforce local laws, called ordinances in the United States. In no case, though, do they possess sovereign powers: that is, powers which they may exercise independently without authorization from a higher authority.

The United States

TERRITORIAL SUBDIVISIONS. In the United States, each state is divided into counties and each county into townships, though some states use other designations. In New England, the county is little more than an area of jurisdiction for the principal state court of first instance, though some of the New England States have given the county a few other functions. In this area, practically all the work of local administration is done by the township or, as it is called in New England, the town. In New York, and some states to the west of it, both counties and townships have local government functions, with the town the more important. In Pennsylvania and a majority of the states in the northern half of the country, the county has the more important functions, but the townships have some. In the southern states, the county does almost all the local work. There the townships are only election districts with no officers of their own except, in some states, justices of the peace. In a few states, part of the state follows one of these plans and part of it another.

There is always a popularly elected county board, known by different names in different states, which manages county affairs in matters in which the state law permits the county any discretionary power. In states where the townships are important, the county board is usually large and is made up of representatives of the townships. Elsewhere, it is usually small, three to seven members, elected either from the county at large or from special districts. The county board can levy taxes and appropriate money for county purposes, but only in the relatively few chartered counties does it have limited power to enact ordinances. Where townships are functional, there is also a township board. In New England, this is a board of selectmen which is merely an executive committee of the town meeting. It carries out decisions of the annual town meeting and may call special town meetings. It supervises town administration, but has very little discretionary power. Administrative officers of counties and townships are usually elected by popular vote as nominees of political parties.

CITIES. Cities always have charters making them municipal corporations and granting them limited powers of self government. In most states outside New England, even small villages are similarly incorporated. A century ago, the state legislature granted a special charter to each individual city, but now charters are all granted under general law. The state ordinarily divides cities into classes according to size, and frequently prescribes exactly the same form of charter for all cities in a size class. Sometimes a city is permitted to choose between two types of charters. More and more states are granting cities above a specified size what is called the home rule privilege. This means that the city may adopt and amend its own charter without direct approval from the state authorities. Even home rule charters, though, must conform in all respects to state laws.

There are three general plans of city government in the United States; the mayor and council plan, the commission plan, and the manager plan. Each is subject to many variations in detail. The mayor and council plan is the old traditional arrangement. It is based on the separation of powers principle and is, in general, a miniature version of the national or state government, the mayor (who is always elected by direct popular vote) standing in much the same relation to the city council that the President does to Congress or the Governor to the state legislature. In the "strong mayor" variety, the mayor appoints most of the administrative officers of the city and has considerable control over city finances. In the "weak mayor" version, the administrative officers are elected, either by popular vote or by the council, and the mayor's influence on finance is limited to making recommendations and the power to veto appropriations. In practice, we find many city governments that come somewhere between these extremes.

The commission plan was much in favor several decades ago, but is now losing ground to the manager plan. Under the commission plan, the voters of the city elect three, five or seven commissioners from the city at large for rotating terms. Each commissioner is the head of an administrative department and all of them together form both the city council and a plural executive. One of them has the title of mayor but, except for representing the city on ceremonial occasions and presiding at meetings of the commission, his position is no different from that of the other commissioners. In practice, there are a great many variations.

In the manager plan, which is now gaining rapidly in favor, the voters elect a city council which, in turn, selects a city manager. The manager is a professional administrator and is supposed to be strictly non-partisan. His function is the efficient management of the city's business. He is responsible to the council, which may dismiss him at any time. Subject to this responsibility, he has complete control of city administration. He appoints the administrative officers and hires lesser employees, usually under a merit system. There is usually a figurehead mayor who represents the city ceremonially, presides over the council, and acts as public relations spokesman for the city government. Some larger cities, wishing to preserve the policy making role of the mayor and at the same time have the benefits of the manager plan, have set up what is called a chief administrative officer. He is appointed by and is responsible to the mayor, but he has the same qualifications and performs the same functions as a city manager.

Great Britain

THE HISTORICAL BACKGROUND. Anglo-Saxon England was divided into shires, which the Norman conquerers renamed counties. The head of the shire was a hereditary earl, but the King's interests were looked after by the sheriff (shire reeve) appointed by the crown. There was also a shiremoot or shire court, consisting of all the free landholders, which acted as both a court of justice and a deliberative body. William the Conquerer took away the powers of the earl, who became a feudal lord, and added a lord lieutenant (at first called a *vicomte*) as commander of the county militia. Later, when the sheriff had become so identified with the local interest of the county that he no longer represented the royal interests, the office of coroner was created as special representative of the Crown. In the fourteenth century, justices of the peace were created, also appointed by the Crown, and county management was given to their Court of Quarter Sessions. This arrangement remained with little change until 1888. As towns grew up in the later middle ages, they obtained charters from the Crown as boroughs (in England, a town is called a city only if it has a cathedral of the Church of England or is designated a city in its charter), but there was no uniformity of pattern.

COUNTIES. An act of Parliament in 1888, called the Local Government Act, with some later additions and amendments, created the present scheme of county government. The historic counties were left undisturbed with the same appointive officers, but today they serve only as judicial districts, election districts and post office addresses. The sheriff, along with some ceremonial functions, has about the same duties as his American counterpart, and also acts as returning officer of elections. The lord lieutenant has some ceremonial duties and nominates men to be appointed justices of the peace. The coroner has been transferred to the administrative county with the same functions as an American coroner. The historic subdivisions of the county, the township and hundred, had long since disappeared and the parish, once a governmental subdivision, had become only an ecclesiastical area. There are no elective offices in the historic county.

ADMINISTRATIVE COUNTIES. The act of 1888 superimposed administrative counties on the historic counties. In most cases, the boundaries are the same, though some of the larger historic counties are divided into two or more administrative counties. The Administrative County of London contains parts of four historic counties. Voters of the county elect, in single member districts, a number of councillors varying with the population of the county. The councillors then elect a number of aldermen equal to one third of their own number. These may be chosen from their own membership or from outside. When a councillor is made an alderman, a special election is held in his district to fill the vacancy. Councillors serve a term of three years; aldermen, six, with one half retiring each three years. Aldermen and councillors sit together as a single body, and elect their chairman. They meet regularly four times a year, but may also have special meetings. They manage county affairs generally, and have limited legislative power. For supervising administration, each council has at least twelve standing committees, each for one aspect of administration, and these committees meet frequently. The actual work of administration is done by non-political county officials. These officials are not formally under a merit system, but they are chosen for their special qualifications and are rarely changed. Each administrative county is divided into several rural districts and urban districts, each with an elective council to manage certain strictly local matters. The county council has general authority over the rural districts which, in many ways, correspond to American townships. The urban districts, which differ from boroughs mainly in that they are smaller and do not have charters, are independent of the county council and have almost the same powers as boroughs.

BOROUGHS. Order was brought out of the chaos of borough government by the Municipal Councils Act of 1835. It is obvious that the county arrangement set up in 1888 followed closely the model of borough government. The voters of the borough (or city, if it happens to be entitled to be called a city) elect a number of councillors depending on the population. Larger boroughs are divided into wards, like an American city, and the councillors are elected by wards. As in the counties, the councillors elect a third as many aldermen as there are councillors, either from their own membership or from outside, and special elections are held to replace councillors promoted to aldermen. Also as in the counties, aldermen serve six-year terms, rotated so that half retire each three years when new councillors are elected. Aldermen and councillors sit together as a single body. They elect the mayor, usually but not always one of their own members. The mayor of an English borough represents the community ceremonially and presides over the council, but has no executive powers. The borough council has about the same legislative and financial powers as an American city council. In addition, it supervises administration through its standing committees. As in the counties, these committees only supervise and make policy, leaving the actual work of administration to non-political administrative officials selected by the full borough council on the basis of special qualifications.

COUNTY BOROUGHS. Most of the larger boroughs are also administrative counties, and are known as county boroughs. In these, the borough council and administrative staff handle matters that are county responsibilities, as well as strictly municipal matters. There are a few cities in the United States that are also counties, but they usually have separate elective county officers distinct from the municipal administrators.

LONDON. What we know as London is an urban complex. At its core is the ancient City of London, with only a few thousand inhabitants, still operating under its medieval charter with a Lord Mayor (who has much prestige but little power) and three councils. Surrounding it, but not including it, is the Administrative County of London which includes the City of Westminster (the real national capital) and twenty-seven boroughs. Each of these has its borough council, which follows the usual pattern and has the usual powers of a non-county borough. The London County Council is like other county councils, but larger. Besides handling the usual county matters, it is a metropolitan government over the whole area with authority over all municipal matters, except police, that are area-wide in scope. Finally, including the county and a great deal larger area outside it (but not the City of London) is the London Metropolitan Police district, directed by a police commissioner and assistants appointed by the Crown on recommendation of the home secretary, a cabinet minister.

RELATION OF LOCAL AND CENTRAL GOVERNMENT. All of these local government units exist under the authority of acts of Parliament and are subject to administrative control. Each department head in the national government has supervisory authority at the local level in matters that pertain to his department. Moreover, to a much greater extent than in the

United States, the national government subsidizes local operations through grants-in-aid. Besides, the national government has a number of boards and commissions that administer special matters, such as electric power, public health and education, at the local level in close cooperation with the local authorities.

OTHER PARTS OF GREAT BRITAIN. The local government arrangements we have been sketching apply specifically only to England and Wales. Scotland, Northern Ireland and even the Republic of Ireland have very similar local government institutions, but they differ in some details from those of England.

France

THE FRENCH REVOLUTION AND NAPOLEON. Long before the French Revolution that began in 1789, the historic French provinces, which had once been almost independent feudal principalities, had lost their importance as areas of government, though they still held the primary loyalty of their people. The country was divided into administrative districts, called "generalities," each governed by an intendant as agent of the king. The ancient communes, which might be anything from tiny peasant villages to large cities, still existed, but had lost any self government they ever had and were governed by a helter-skelter assortment of royal agents. One of the first acts of the revolutionary National Assembly in 1789 was to abolish the provinces and generalities. France was divided into more than eighty areas called *departments,* corresponding roughly to the English counties. Each *department* was divided into several *arrondissements,* and each *arrondissement* into the ancient communes. At each level, the people were to govern themselves through elected councils. The people were not ready for self government, so the result was confusion. Partly to remedy this confusion, but mainly because he wished to centralize all power in his own hands, Napoleon abolished this local self government and substituted a hierarchy of officials appointed by the central government. Over each *department* he placed a prefect, and over each *arrondissement,* a subprefect. Even the mayors of the communes were appointed by the central government.

LOCAL GOVERNMENT TODAY. The general framework of this structure has persisted through the two empires, two kingdoms, four republics, and one fascist regime that France has had since 1800. Under the third and fourth republics, elective councils were restored at all three local levels, and the communes were permitted to elect their mayor. However, the councils had little more than advisory power, and the prefect and subprefect still managed local affairs under directions from Paris. Even the mayors of the communes acted chiefly as agents of the central government.

The constitution of the Fifth Republic declares that the communes and *departments* "shall be free to govern themselves through elected councils and under conditions stipulated by law." The prefect remains. Officially his title has been changed to "delegate of the government," but he is still commonly called prefect. The constitution states that he "shall be responsible for the national interests, for administrative supervision, and for seeing that the laws are respected." The *arrondissement* is not mentioned in the new constitution, but it had already become only a minor administrative district like the Southern township in the United States. It still survives in that capacity. There is another subdivision, the canton, which comes between the commune and the arrondissement, but it has no government functions. It is, as it has been for more than a century, merely a judicial district for minor courts and an election district for members of *arrondissement* and *department* council members. Some progress was made in democratizing local government under the Fourth Republic, and more is being made under the Fifth Republic.

THE DEPARTMENT. The French *department,* like the British or American county, is the principal unit of local government and administration, but that is about as far as the similarity goes. They are under much greater control by the central government, have much less freedom of action, and much more limited financial resources. They can collect some local taxes, but not a general property tax. They get grants-in-aid from the national government for certain purposes, but they must pay the local costs of many activities of the central government.

THE PREFECT. Although less of a local monarch than he once was, the prefect, or delegate of the government, is still the dominant figure in the *department*. He is appointed by the President of the Republic on recommendation of the cabinet, which really means the recommendation of the Minister of the Interior. In all of his work he is responsible to the Minister of the Interior. Strictly speaking, he is not a member of the civil service; in fact, many of his functions are political. Even so, he is a career official who may be transferred from one *department* to another, but is almost never removed. He has a triple role: administrative agent of the central government, spokesman for his *department* with the national authorities, and semi-independent executive of the *department*.

He is chief administrator of the *department* and appoints the administrative officers, though most of these are now covered by the merit system. He initiates all legislation by the council which touches national interest or national policy. He has what amounts to a veto on other acts of the council, except the budget, in that he can refuse to execute any act which he considers contrary to national interest or national policy. He prepares the budget and submits it to the council. The council, though, like an American legislature, is not bound to accept or reject the budget entire, but may change any item not made mandatory by national law. Besides, the prefect is expected to be a sort of paternal guardian of the welfare of all citizens of his *department*, even intervening in the courts in their behalf or carrying their problems to the ministry in Paris.

THE DEPARTMENT COUNCIL. Each *department* has an elective council of a size depending on the population of the *department*. Members are elected, at least one from each commune, for six-year terms, half of them retiring every three years. The council elects its president, who also has some limited executive functions, though he can always be overruled by the prefect. The council meets twice a year and may be called into special session. Between sessions, an interim committee performs the routine functions of the council.

The most important independent function of the *department* council is to vote the budget. Only on items required by national law (mainly the cost of national government activities in the department) may the prefect spend money which the council has not appropriated. It legislates on matters presented to it by the prefect, but this amounts to little more than giving formal assent to things that will be done anyway. The council can legislate on its own initiative on some local matters, chiefly providing health, recreational and welfare facilities. Beyond these limited powers, the council is a spokesman for its constituents with the national government. By resolution, it may request the prefect to present any matter to the Minister of the Interior, and he almost always complies. Moreover, it is not uncommon for members of either house of the national parliament to be at the same time members of a *department* council (they also often serve as mayors or councillors of the communes), and this provides a ready-made lobby at the source of power.

THE ARRONDISSEMENTS. Each *arrondissement* has a subprefect, who is merely an agent of the prefect of the *department*, and an elective council. The rural *arrondissement* is only an administrative subdivision with no independent powers. However, a number of urban *arrondissements* have been made into what amounts to municipalities with mayors, assistant mayors, councils and administrators like the larger communes. This device is used where a number of historic communes, each too small to provide municipal services, have grown together into an urban complex in which such services are needed. A movement is also under way to combine groups of rural *arrondissements* into special districts to provide certain services.

COMMUNES. Historically, French communes derive from medieval feudal manors. Originally, each was a manorial village and the surrounding fields. Today, like New England towns, they are territorial subdivisions, each extending to where the next begins. Each contains at least a small village, and sometimes a large urban community, but there is no separate government for the village and the surrounding country. One difference between the New England town and the French commune is that, in New England, when an urban community reaches a certain size, varying from state to state, it may become chartered as a city. There are no chartered cities in France. A French city is either a large commune or an urban *arrondissement*.

Each commune or urban *arrondissement* has an elective council of a size varying with the population. The council elects a mayor and, except in the smallest communes, one or more adjoints or assistant mayors. These act as administrative officials under the mayor's direction. In the largest communes and the urban *arrondissements* there are also permanent administrators who are in the national civil service. The mayor is both president of the council and a semi-independent executive.

The amount of municipal self-government varies with the size of the commune. In the larger cities, the mayor and council have almost as much freedom of action as in an American city, though their acts may always be overruled by national authorities. The mayor must still act as representative of the national government, but he is no longer restricted to that role as he was in earlier times. The council must always face the possibility that its acts may be overruled by the prefect of the *department*. There is no separation of powers. The mayor is a member of the council, as well as its presiding officer. He may take part in its debates and vote on all measures, but he has no veto. The position of mayor of a large commune carries great prestige, out of all proportion to the powers of the office. Like the *departments,* the larger communes have a tie-in with the national government in that the mayor and several councillors are apt to be members of parliament. This duality of office holding is not prohibited in France as it is in common law countries.

PARIS. Like most national capitals, Paris has special arrangements and is under more direct control by the national government than other parts of the country. The Commune of Paris, or Paris proper, has a municipal council of 90 members, elected by wards under proportional representation. The council elects its own president, but he is not a mayor. Greater Paris, the city and its suburbs, coincides almost exactly with the Department of the Seine. The commune councillors meet with sixty more from the suburbs as a department council. However, there are two prefects, the Prefect of the Seine and the Prefect of Police, who represent the national ministry and have all executive and administrative authority. The councils can deliberate and petition, but have almost no municipal legislative power.

West Germany

THE LÄNDER. As previously noted, the official name of West Germany is the Federal Republic of Germany, and we have been treating it as a true federal union. Actually, though, it is only quasi-federal. It consists of ten *Länder* (lands) or as we should call them states, each with its own constitution and government. However, the central government has concurrent authority with the lands and may overrule almost any of their acts. Each *Land* has a "state legislature" called a *Landtag*, unicameral except in Bavaria, whose members are popularly elected under proportional representation, in most *Länder* for four year terms. Each *Landtag* elects a minister-president, who is a combination of state governor and prime minister, and a cabinet of ministers, each of whom heads an administrative department. Ministerial responsibility varies. In Hesse, the *Landtag* can force the cabinet out at any time by a vote of censure; in Bavaria, the ministers can not be forced to resign at all; in most of the *Länder*, there are restrictions on the power of the *Landtag* to force a resignation of the cabinet. The *Landtag* can legislate on almost any matter so long as its acts do not conflict with national law. The tendency is, though, to leave general legislation to the national parliament while the *Landtag* acts only in matters of strictly local concern. As in most cabinet type governments, there is no executive veto. The *Landtag* also devotes much time to the discussion of national issues. Its cabinet ministers, or at least some of them, are members of the national *Bundesrat* so the *Landtag* can, by resolution, instruct them how to vote in that body, just as, in pre-Civil War days in the United States, state legislatures often instructed United States Senators how to vote in the Senate.

KREISE. Each German *Land* is divided into *Kreise*, a word that literally means circle, but is usually translated county. These are the principal units of local government. Like English counties and French *departments*, they are both areas of local administration for the *Land* government and partially self governing communities. They enjoy less freedom of action than English counties, but more than French *departments*. They are of two classes, rural and urban. Rural counties have an elected assembly (*Kreistag*), chosen by proportional representation, which elects an executive council and a chief county administrator called a *Landrat*. Each town or village in the county has its own local government with an elected council, or in very small ones, a town meeting, and a mayor or *Bürgermeister*. The *Landrat*, sometimes translated county manager, and his assistants are professional administrators and members of the civil service of the state. There are also agents of the state (*Land*) government to administer local services of the state. Usually state and county officials work in close cooperation.

The urban county differs from the rural in that it is also a city, thus resembling the English county boroughs. In the urban counties, members of the council, which functions for both city and county matters, are elected by proportional representation, usually for four year terms. They choose a mayor (*Bürgermeister*) for a longer term than their own, and also a group of administrative assistants called the *Magistrat* or magistracy. In cities of more than 10,000 population, the mayor is called an *Oberbürgermeister* (overmayor) and his chief assistant in the *Magistrat* has the title of *Bürgermeister*. All of these are professional administrators and members of the state civil service. Although he is ceremonial head of the city and is responsible for executing the ordinances passed by the council, a *Bürgermeister* is more like an American city

manager than an American mayor. He is strictly non-political
and is often hired away from one city by another.

GERMAN CITIES. The German city (*Stadt*), whether an
urban county or a town in a rural county, has a separate existence of its own. In this respect, it is like a British or American city, but unlike one in France. Like cities everywhere, it is
subject to a great deal of state control, and many of its functions are made mandatory by state law. It never has what
Americans call "home rule"; the form of its government is
prescribed by state law and, except for somewhat more complex administrative arrangements in larger places, is the same
for cities of all sizes. Its independent taxing powers are strictly
limited, but it receives a portion of the state and national
taxes paid by its citizens. The typical German city operates
a wide variety of municipal enterprises. Besides those frequently operated by American cities, such as electric service,
water supply, local public transportation, health services and
parks, it usually runs municipal theaters, municipal markets,
pawnshops, and even slaughter houses. The earnings of these
enterprises form an important part of the city's revenue.

REGIERUNGSBEZIRKE. Some of the states or *Länder* have
another administrative area between the state government and
the counties. It is called a *Regierungsbezirk* which may be
translated, almost literally, government district. It is strictly
an administrative unit and not an area of self government. Its
official personnel consists of a district president, an administrative board, and a district committee, all appointed by the
state minister of the interior, and members of the state civil
service, all of whom are agents of the state government.
Where these districts exist, they perform some of the state
administrative functions that otherwise would fall to officials
of the counties.

EAST GERMANY. East Germany, called officially the
German Democratic Republic, has five *Länder* and almost the
same local government scheme as West Germany. On paper,
its local government is even more democratic, leaving much

wider powers to the county and city councils. This is only an empty form, though, because these councils, like all other organs of government, are controlled by the Communist and pro-Communist political groups.

Italy

GENERAL FEATURES. The pattern of local government in the Republic of Italy is, in most respects, a return to the pattern that prevailed in the Kingdom of Italy in pre-Fascist days. Except for the areas called regions, this pattern was copied deliberately from the French, with provinces corresponding to the French *departments,* and communes that were about the same as the communes in France. The nearest thing to the *arrondissements* are special administrative districts that were created in some provinces, but not in all.

The republic has given more democratic self government to the subdivisions than they had under the monarchy, with a remarkably uniform structure. At each level there is a popularly elected unicameral council, whose members serve four year terms. This council elects an executive committee and a presiding officer. At each level there is also an official who represents the national interest with some control over the elective council.

THE REGIONS. The regions were originally the separate states (or major divisions of them) which were combined into the Kingdom of Italy a century ago. After unification, they were, like the historic French provinces, deprived of all governmental functions, though the old names continued to be used to designate areas. The constitution of the republic provides for reviving the regions, nineteen of them, as government units. In each, a regional council is· to be elected by popular vote. This council is to elect an executive committee (*giunta*), and a regional president who is to perform the routine functions of a chief executive. The council is also to draft a regional constitution, which must be approved by the national parliament, and this constitution may authorize the council to levy certain taxes, spend money for regional functions, and legislate on regional matters that do not interfere with national interests. To represent these national interests, there is to be a commissioner, appointed by and responsible to the Minister of the Interior. He is to administer national functions in the region, coordinate national and local administration, and may, on direction of the national government, exercise a suspensive veto on acts of the council. If the council repasses the act by an absolute majority, it may be referred to the national parliament for final action, or to the Constitutional Court, if its legality is questioned.

The regional commissioners exist in all the regions to manage national affairs at that level, but the regional councils have been set up in less than half the regions. The initiative in implementing this provision of the constitution must be taken by the national government by calling an election in a particular region to elect a council. The national government has been slow to act, probably fearing that the Communists would gain control in some critical regions. Whether regionalism, as a timid step toward federalism, is to die on the vine, is still an unsettled question in Italy.

THE PROVINCES. Like the French *department* or the British county, the province is the chief unit of local government, especially for rural areas. In each province, there is a prefect who, like his French counterpart, is appointed by and responsible to the Minister of the Interior. Under the monarchy, as under the Third Republic in France, the prefect dominated his province, with the elective council having little more than advisory power. Now, as in France, his powers have been curtailed somewhat, giving the council and its officers much more freedom of action. The prefect may still issue orders to the provincial president (or the mayors of the communes) on some matters, and may dissolve the council on orders from the Minister of the Interior, for reasons of national security, and assume complete power. The prefect is also subject to directives from the regional commissioner. In the early days of the republic, it was often assumed that the powers and functions of the prefect would be transferred, step by step, to the regional commissioners, and that the office of prefect would disappear. At present, there is no trend in that direction.

THE COMMUNES. The Italian communes are much like the communes in France. They are territorial subdivisions, centering around a village, town or city which has no separate government, and their functions are mainly municipal. In smaller communes, the president of the council is the head of the community. Larger communes have an elective mayor who, in addition to the usual functions of a mayor, represents the national interests and is responsible to the prefect of the province. Each member of the executive committee in the commune (as in the province and the organized region) heads an administrative division, and is responsible to the council for his administrative acts.

The Soviet Union

TERRITORIAL ORGANIZATION. The Russian Socialist Federated Soviet Republic, which is several times larger than all the other fourteen union republics combined, is divided into territories (*Krais*) and autonomous republics. Each of these, and each of the other union republics, is divided into regions (*oblasts*), which are the principal units of administrative control. The *oblast* is divided into districts (*raions*), corresponding roughly to counties. Each *raion* usually contains several villages and small towns, which are subject to its authority. Larger cities may be likened to county boroughs. They are not subject to the *raion* in which they are located geographically, but are under the supervision of the *oblast*. Some very large cities are not even under the *oblast* in which they are located, but are directly subject to the authority of the union republic.

THE SOVIETS. Soviet is the Russian word for council, and formally, the Union of Socialist Soviet Republics, or the Soviet Union for short, is ruled by a pyramid of soviets or councils from the lowest to the highest level. We have already discussed the Supreme Soviet of the Union. Except in small villages, where its place is taken by a town meeting, each of the units mentioned in the last paragraph has a soviet elected by the voters. In the *raions* and smaller cities, the "deputies" (members of the council) are elected for two-year terms; in the *oblasts* and larger cities, for three-year terms; in the autonomous republics and union republics, for four-year terms. The councils are all large, and each divides into committees for each field of administration. Each council elects administrative officers and each of the larger has an executive committee or presidium which can act on behalf of the whole council. At each level, the council is subject to directives and vetoes from the council of the next higher level but, with this limitation, it is supposed to manage most governmental and economic affairs in its own area. All, except the Supreme Soviet of the Union, are unicameral.

All of this may sound democratic, but it is not so by Western standards. To begin with, the election of council members gives the voter no choice. The candidates are hand picked by Communist party agencies, and there is only one candidate for each position. Then when the council elects its committees (or sections as they are also called), its administrators, and its presidium (if it has one), it only goes through the motions of approving selections made by higher authorities or by Communist party agencies. As one writer puts it, the council is ruled by its executive which in turn is ruled by higher authorities. The council can discuss and sometimes complain, but it has no real power to act. The arrangement helps to keep the people satisfied and gives them a sense of participation, but it does not change the fact that in the Soviet Union all power rests with the presidium of the All Union Communist Party and that policy decisions at all lower levels are made in accordance with directives from this all powerful group. Anyone who digresses from the "party line" gets into trouble with the political police.

Other Countries

DIVERSITY. No two countries have exactly the same local government arrangements. Most of them resemble rather closely some one or some combination of those already described. Most of the newly emerging nations follow, with some variation, the local government plans of the countries of which they were formerly dependencies. Here we can glance briefly at only a few of them.

AUSTRIA. Present day Austria, which has some of the features of federalism, is divided into provinces, each with an elective governor and unicameral assembly. The governor, along with being the ceremonial head of the province, is the chief provincial officer in the administration of national affairs, and provincial prime minister. Cities have much the same arrangements as in West Germany.

BELGIUM. Belgium retains its nine historic provinces as the principal units of local government and administration. The provincial governor is a political official, chosen by the Minister of the Interior, and changes with political changes in the national cabinet. He is primarily an administrative agent of the national government, but he also executes acts of the provincial council. Members of this unicameral council are elected for four-year terms, and they elect a "permanent deputation," which is the provincial cabinet. The province is divided into *arrondissements*, similar in nature and functions to the French *arrondissements*, and communes. Each commune has a burgomaster, aldermen and council, who perform the usual functions of municipal government. Acts of the commune may be overridden by the national government.

JAPAN. Japan is divided into forty-six prefectures, each of which is divided into cities, towns and villages. Before World War II, the prefecture was ruled by a prefect appointed by the Emperor, with an elective council which had only advisory power. Under the present constitution, the prefecture enjoys a large measure of self-government, with a unicameral council, whose members are elected for four-year terms, and an elected governor. The subdivisions, like the French communes, are territorial units, with no separate government for the city, town or village and the surrounding countryside. Each has an elective mayor and council. The police, who handle most matters of national administration at the local level, are under the National Public Safety Commission of five members, appointed for staggered terms by the Prime Minister. Not more than two of them can be of the same political party.

NORWAY. Norway is divided into twenty counties, each of which (except Oslo and Bergen which are county boroughs) is divided into rural and urban districts. Each district has an elective unicameral council, which chooses one fourth of its members as a "presidency," or district executive. Chairmen of the district councils form the county council.

SWEDEN. Sweden is divided into twenty-five administrative districts, each called a *lan*. Each *lan* has a governor, appointed by the King on recommendation of the cabinet, and an elective legislature called a *lansting*. Each *lan* is divided into parishes with local self-government.

SWITZERLAND. Switzerland being a true federal union, each canton may adopt its own constitution, the only national requirement being that each have a republican form of government. Consequently, there is considerable variation. Some small rural cantons have "direct democracy." Taxes are levied, money appropriated, and laws enacted in a primary assembly of all adult male citizens. They elect an executive board, usually of five members, which manages affairs between assemblies. The larger cantons usually have a popularly elected unicameral council and a plural executive. In some cantons, the executive board is elected by the council; in others, it is elected directly by the voters. Some of the largest cantons are divided into administrative districts, similar to the French *arrondissements*, each under a prefect who is responsible to the canton. All cantons are divided into communes. Here something has been done that resembles the arrangement of English counties. The historic communes remain, with few if any government functions, but superimposed are "political" communes, which provide the municipal self-government with elective mayors and councils or, in the smaller ones, town meetings.

Suggested Questions for Discussion

1. What is meant by the term "local government"? Does it necessarily include self government for the local units?
2. What difference does it make in the functions and responsibilities of local government whether a country is a unitary state or a federal union?
3. Describe comparatively the divisions and subdivisions of several countries as local government units.
4. Several countries have prefects or similar officers as links between central and local governments. How is this relationship handled in other countries?
5. Compare the status of, and the self-government arrangements for, urban communities in the major countries.
6. What is the English "county borough"? In what other countries is something similar to it found?
7. What is meant by saying that local government units are "creatures of a sovereign state"?
8. What are the principal plans of municipal government found in the United States? What are the advantages of each? In what other countries are arrangements found that are similar to any of these plans?
9. What are the principal activities in which municipal governments engage in the various countries?
10. Why do national capitals usually have different government arrangements than other cities in the same country? What are the arrangements in: (1) Washington; (2) London; (3) Paris?
11. What is meant by saying that local government units are always administrative divisions of a country or of component units of a federal union?
12. Evaluate the provision for regions and regional governments in Italy.

Bibliography

Anderson, W., Ed., Local Government in Europe (New York, 1939)

Chapman, B., Introduction to French Local Government (London, 1953)

Finer, H., English Local Government (London, 1950)

Gillen, J. F. G., State and Local Government in West Germany, 1945-1953 (Berlin, Office of U.S. High Commissioner, 1953)

Hadfield, E. C. R., and MacColl, J. E., British Local Government (New York, 1949)

Munro, W. B., Government of European Cities (New York, 1927)

Functions of Government

Varying Theories

TRADITIONAL FUNCTIONS. There are certain things that governments of sovereign states always have done and still do. These may be called the traditional functions of government. They include such things as maintaining order, defining and punishing crimes, and settling disputes among their citizens or subjects. They almost always maintain a military force to defend their realms against attack and to suppress revolts and rebellions. They issue money and prescribe standards of weights and measures. They raise funds by taxation or other means to meet their operating expenses.

GOVERNMENT AND ECONOMICS. In one way or another, and to one degree or another, governments have always been involved in the economic processes, and consequently in the social order of their realms. Whether so intended or not, taxes have an effect on business and trade. Laws governing land tenure and inheritance affect economic conditions. In ancient and medieval times the granting of charters to guilds and the confirming of privileges to certain social classes influenced the pattern of economic life profoundly. More often than not, governments have provided some kind of social services, at least poor relief. For the past two centuries, practically all governments have provided postal service. Even the coining of money and the standardization of weights and measures are in the nature of economic services to the community.

It is in this area of the relation of government to economic processes and the social structure that we find the real disagreement as to the proper functions of government. Often this disagreement is the root of political issues and even of international conflicts. There are various theories as to what the role of government should be.

MERCANTILISM. From the beginning of modern times until the days of the American and French revolutions, all governments of Western Europe were committed to what was called the mercantile theory or mercantilism. This doctrine held that the government should regulate the economic processes in the interest of national prosperity. Believing that only gold and silver are real wealth, government controls were aimed at bringing large stocks of these precious metals into the country. Foreign trade especially was regulated to encourage exports and discourage imports, so that the difference would have to be paid in gold and silver. This was called a favorable balance of trade, a term which we still use. Different countries applied mercantilism in different ways. Spain used it to exploit her American colonies. In France, along with strict regulation of foreign trade, it also took the form of applying government pressure to increase production, so that France would have more goods to export. Britain was concerned mainly with assuring the profits of her merchants and excluding foreigners from competition with them. Since trade with the British colonies in America was highly profitable, they were subjected to few mercantilist restrictions until the eve of the revolution.

We no longer talk of mercantilism and we no longer consider gold and silver the only real wealth. However, in the modified form of economic nationalism, mercantilism is still very much alive. Governments regulate foreign trade and subsidize the industries of their own countries, through "tax incentives" and otherwise, to promote national prosperity. They "protect" home industries with tariffs, import quotas, and other trade restrictions. They engage in extensive activities to find foreign markets for their exports. If they are short of capital, they try to bring in foreign investments, but often under conditions that make such investments unattractive.

LAISSEZ FAIRE. With the beginning of the industrial revolution, a new theory arose called *laissez faire* (also spelled *laisser faire*). Translated literally, it means "leave be," but the usual free translation is "let alone." It would have the government keep its hands off the economic processes entirely and leave control to such economic principles as the law of supply and demand. The term was coined by a group of French economists, called the Physiocrats, late in the eighteenth century, but it was popularized by the Scottish economist Adam Smith in his book *The Wealth of Nations*, published in the same year as the American Declaration of Independence. Smith was protesting against mercantilism. He objected especially to restrictions on international trade, such as protective tariff duties. He believed that the wealth of nations — all nations — would be increased if each country should produce only what it could produce most economically and trade freely with other countries which could produce other commodities to better advantage.

Complete *laissez faire*, therefore, would limit the role of government to the traditional functions, leaving the regulation of all economic processes to the free play of competition. During the nineteenth century, practically all business people professed faith in the doctrine, but most of them had some mental reservations. In most countries, industrialists and merchants wanted no government regulation of their business, but they insisted on tariff protection and were often seeking government subsidies in one form or another. In the United States, the early canals were built either by the states or with the help of state subsidies. Most of the railroads received federal land grants and federal or state loans, which were never repaid. Great Britain, for several decades, allowed free international trade (tariff duties were levied only for revenue), but even there government intervention was necessary to protect the workers. Today we seldom hear the term *laissez faire* and probably few people believe that it would be possible under present day conditions, but many still hold it as an ideal and wish to hold government regulation and control to an absolute minimum.

SOCIALISM. It is difficult to define socialism because different people use the word to mean different things. To Russians, it means totalitarian state capitalism. To some persons who lean strongly to the *laissez faire* ideal, any government participation in the economic process is socialism. To most people who call themselves socialists, the term implies some measure of "nationalization" or government operation of industry. The word socialism was first used, at least in the English language, by Robert Owen, whom we usually associate with the ill starred utopian experiment at New Harmony, Indiana. Owen was a British mill owner who became disturbed by the plight of his workers and turned his attention to seeking ways to raise the living standards of all workers. In a book, *A New View of Society,* published in 1814, he used the word socialism to describe the scheme of cooperative workers communities which he advocated. A generation later, the economic philosopher John Stuart Mill adopted the term. In his book, *Principles of Political Economy,* published in 1848, he used it to describe his ideal of "the greatest good to the greatest number." Both of these men were fully committed to the free enterprise system, merely favoring limited government action to bring about what they considered a fairer distribution of the benefits.

For the past century, socialism has been associated with the doctrines of Karl Marx. We can not, in this brief space, undertake a real analysis of Marxism. He began by interpreting history as a record of the exploitation of the masses by the classes, with luxury for the privileged few and misery for the many. As time moved on, one order of society had become outworn and given way to another, which in turn had had its span and broken down. Thus the slave economy of the ancient world had given way to feudalism. Feudalism had run its course and been replaced by capitalism. Now capitalism was ready to give way to socialism. This Marxian socialism was to be a classless society, in which everyone would be a worker, and production would be for the common good of all. The capitalist class, with private investment and the private ownership of industry, would be eliminated. All industry would be run by and for the workers. He was not clear how this was to be done, but his followers have usually interpreted it to mean that all industry should be operated by government, and that the working class should control the government.

In Free World countries, socialist parties (which usually call themselves "Social Democratic" parties) are for democracy and against totalitarianism. They usually advocate the nationalization of basic industries and the operation of these industries, not for profit, but to provide a maximum of goods and services at a minimum price. Few if any Free World socialists favor the entire elimination of private enterprise and they are usually willing to cooperate with other parties (through coalition cabinets) in supporting "welfare state" programs.

The Russians and their satellites have produced their own version of Marxian socialism under the name of Communism. In its literal meaning, communism would eliminate all property, and all buying and selling. Everything would be owned in common. Each would work according to his ability and receive according to his needs. Obviously this does not exist in the Soviet Union. The government operates all business and all industry, but operates it for profit. It uses the profit to maintain its military establishment and its apparatus for intrigue and propaganda. There is a money economy. People work for wages and buy what they have the money to buy — if it is available. Workers are "exploited" far worse than in capitalistic countries. Their wages are set by the government; they can not bargain collectively and they can not strike. They work longer hours for a smaller return than workers in any other industrialized country.

Perhaps the nearest we can come to summarizing the socialist theory of the functions of government is to say that, according to socialism, it is a function of government to see that goods and services are made available to the consumer at a reasonable cost; that whenever, because of the basic character of the industry or for some other special reason, private enterprise fails to meet this condition, it is within the proper sphere of government to take over and operate these industries. Obviously, the line between the socialist theory and the "welfare state" theory is hazy.

WELFARE STATE. The welfare state theory of the functions of government differs from the socialist theory in two important particulars. First, it owes nothing to Marxian doctrine. Second, it seeks to preserve the essential features of a capitalistic free enterprise economy and sanctions the government's engaging in economic projects only to supplement private enterprise or in extreme situations where private enterprise is unable or unwilling to undertake projects that are needed for the public welfare. There are two aspects of it, which have different backgrounds. One aspect is the extensive regulation of private enterprise by government. This differs from the old mercantilist regulation in that its goal is the protection of the welfare of workers and consumers, rather than enhancing the profits of producers or accumulating wealth in the country, regardless of how that wealth is distributed. Such regulation came about step by step in Great Britain during the nineteenth century, and the United States began to turn to it in the early 1900's. Most industrialized countries outside the Communist group now practice such regulation, some of them with socialist or mercantilist overtones. The other aspect of the welfare state theory is that government should engage directly in activities to promote the well being of its citizens, such as what we call social security in the United States. To some extent, governments have always engaged in some social welfare activities, such as poor relief, and for the past century most governments have provided public health services. In the 1860's, Napoleon III of France instituted sickness insurance for workers, and in the 1880's Chancellor Bismarck of Germany set up an elaborate social welfare program, under the misleading name of state socialism, which included something very much like our social security. Today, practically all the countries of Western Europe, the older nations of the British Commonwealth, the United States, and a number of other countries act on the welfare state theory to the extent of providing a wide variety of welfare services for their citizens. The theory may be stated as the belief that, within the framework of a free enterprise economy, it is the proper function of government to take whatever action may seem appropriate to provide for the economic and cultural well being of its citizens.

The Scope of Government Functions

AN AGE OF BIG GOVERNMENT. We live in an age of big government. Whatever theory or combination of theories may be followed, and whatever structure governments may have, governments everywhere engage in functions that were undreamed of when the United States became independent. This growing extent and complexity of government functions is an inevitable consequence of other changes that have been taking place. The enormous growth of population, the clustering of people into cities, the growing complexity of society, and the tremendous growth and diversification of industry, largely as a consequence of a spiraling outpouring of inventions, have created myriad problems with which government must cope. As the problems have multiplied and their solutions have become more costly, local government machinery and resources have proved inadequate to meet them, and the people have turned to their national governments to do what needs to be done. Hence, forced to take on new functions, and to enlarge their administrative staffs to get the work done, national governments have all become big governments, with their tentacles reaching into almost every phase of life.

THE HISTORIC POLICE POWER FUNCTION. The police power is almost identical with what we usually call general welfare power. It is sometimes defined as the power to make and enforce laws for the protection of the health, morals, and general welfare of the people. Since the eighteenth century, it has been recognized as one of the inherent powers of sovereignty. In unitary states this power belongs to the national government, which may delegate portions or phases of it to the subdivisions. In some federal unions, it is a concurrent power of both levels, usually with a provision that, in case of conflict, the law of the national government shall prevail. In the United States, it has posed a constitutional problem. It was the intention of the constitution makers to reserve the police power to the states. Although the Constitution twice uses the term general welfare, it does not confer a general welfare power on the central government, and the Tenth Amendment states that all powers not delegated to the United States nor prohibited to the states are reserved to the states. This was well enough in the early days when police power legislation dealt only with public morals, domestic relations, and such public health matters as quarantines and the licensing of physicians. By the beginning of this century, though, many problems had grown beyond the competence of the states, and the federal government began looking for a way to enter the police power field. The way was found by expanding the meaning of the power of Congress to regulate commerce among the states. Beginning with the pure food laws of 1906, the federal government has assumed control over labor relations, the protection of wild life, and many other general welfare matters, all under the guise of regulating interstate commerce.

REGULATORY FUNCTIONS. Police power laws are regulatory in character, but when we think of the regulatory functions of government we usually have in mind the regulation of the economic processes. Such regulation has grown enormously in recent decades in all industrialized countries, and in the United States it has been shifted largely to the federal government under the power to regulate commerce. One problem that has loomed large in most Free World countries, and especially in the United States, is the effort to preserve competition by preventing competing concerns from combining into monopolies. Most governments now set minimum wages and restrict the hours and working conditions of labor. Many practices of business in general have been brought under legal control. Two types of business are under especially stringent controls, usually through special administrative agencies created for the purpose. First are businesses that deal in other people's money, such as banks, stock exchanges and insurance companies. Second are industries that are in the nature of public utilities or, in the language of the common law, "are vested with a public interest." These include railroads, air lines, telecommunications, and other industries on which the public depends for essential services. In the United States, as in most other federal unions, some of this regulation is by the national government and some by the component units.

GOVERNMENT ENTERPRISE. Today, almost all governments engage in some business enterprises. This may be on the basis of socialist theory, or it may be just a matter of expediency. The oldest government enterprise is the post office. In addition to this, often in conjunction with it, most European governments also operate their railroads and their telephone and telegraph lines. Some of them operate their radio and television broadcasting. A number of governments also engage in other lines of business, such as electric power and steel production, often in competition with private enterprise. Most governments operate their central bank which is usually the only agency in the country that can issue currency. The United States government does less of this sort of thing than most national governments, but even we have our Tennessee Valley Authority and other public power enterprises as well as a number of government lending agencies. Both in America and in Europe, local governments frequently operate such public utility enterprises as water supply, electric power and public transportation. Besides, European cities, especially in West Germany, Austria and Italy, commonly operate a municipal theater or municipal opera, and some of them run a variety of local enterprises. As previously noted, in the Soviet Union, all economic enterprises are owned and operated by the government.

Such government enterprise may be directly under the management of a cabinet department, or its equivalent at the local level. This is the usual practice in continental Europe. The English speaking countries prefer to put the management of each industry in the hands of a non-partisan or bi-partisan board or commission, with members appointed for long, rotating terms, to avoid political pressure. Another device used in Britain and the United States is the government corporation.

Thus the British Broadcasting Corporation and the American Home Owners Loan Corporation are entirely government owned, but as corporations they can do business without administrative interference by government officials. Some Latin American countries use a mixed device in which the government holds stock, often a controlling interest, in private corporations. This cuts the government in on management and profits, but still leaves the way open to attract private investment.

SERVICE FUNCTIONS. In almost all countries, including our own, governments at the different levels provide a number of services to their citizens, either free to the user or supplied at merely nominal charges. National governments forecast the weather, and engage in research activities in agriculture, science and economic matters, making their findings available to persons concerned. They usually have programs for the conservation of natural resources. They provide recreational facilities through national parks or similar projects. They may also provide hospitals and other public health services. In Great Britain, the National Health Service undertakes to provide complete medical and hospital care for everyone. Physicians, nurses and other medical personnel are employees of the government and all hospitals are government hospitals. Every wage earner pays a small fee, through payroll deduction, for this service, and the deficit is made up from general taxes. Private medical practice is permitted, and persons who choose to do so may patronize the private physicians, but most people take advantage of the national service.

In the United States, most individual states maintain hospitals for mental cases and sometimes for other diseases. American cities, and sometimes counties, have their own hospitals and clinics, and sometimes visiting nurse service. Much the same is true in most countries of Western Europe. Except in Britain and the Soviet Union, though, these services are free only to persons who can not afford to pay.

Another service undertaken by government in all countries is the building and maintenance of highways, made necessary by the increasing use of the automobile. In most countries, both the central government and the local units build roads, but the major highway system is maintained by the national government. In the United States, the same constitutional problem arose as with the police power. The Constitution does not give our federal government authority to build roads, so the actual building and maintenance is left to the states. However, the federal government gives financial grants to help defray the cost and, by attaching conditions to these grants, it is able to prescribe specifications for major highways.

Still another public service which all governments now provide is education. In France, Italy, and some smaller countries, education at all levels is under the direct administration of the central government through a ministry of education. In Britain, elementary and secondary schools are managed by committees of the county councils in conformity with rigid standards set by the national ministry of education. In the United States, education is one of the powers reserved to the states, though the federal government has granted financial aid in some situations. Arrangements differ in the various states, but in most of them locally elected boards of education operate the elementary and secondary schools, and sometimes junior colleges, with some financial aid from the state and under the general supervision of a state education office.

At the level of higher education, some countries, such as France and Mexico, maintain national universities. In many others, such as Britain and West Germany, the national government gives financial aid to private universities. In the United States and Canada, each state or province usually maintains a university and one or more other colleges, but in both these countries private colleges and universities continue to flourish without financial aid from any government. A recent development in the United States is the municipal university. Several larger cities (and some that are not so large) have such municipal universities.

GRANTS-IN-AID. Grants-in-aid are financial grants from a higher level of government to a lower to aid in meeting the cost of some project or activity. Government grants for one purpose or another have been made throughout recorded history, but grants-in-aid, as the term is now understood, probably began with federal land grants in the United States. Even before the Constitution was adopted, the old Congress of the Confederation, in the Ordinance of 1785, set aside one section of land in each township to be granted to each state that might be formed out of the Northwest Territory for the purpose of providing public schools. During the Civil War, the Morrill Land Grant Act granted public land to every state for the purposes of establishing an agricultural college. These schools are still called land grant colleges. So long as the federal government had plenty of good land, these grants raised no constitutional question, since Congress has power to dispose of federal property. When it became necessary to make money grants, constitutional justification was found in the tax clause. The Constitution says "The Congress shall have power to lay and collect taxes . . . , to pay the debts and provide for the common defense and general welfare of the United States." This was interpreted to mean that, while the United States can not engage directly in general welfare projects, Congress can collect taxes for the purpose and grant the money to the states. Today the federal government grants money to the states for road building, public housing, slum clearance, urban renewal, and many other general welfare activities. We usually speak of this as federal aid. But the states in turn grant money to cities, school districts, and other subdivisions for various purposes.

The term grant-in-aid originated with the British. Around the beginning of the present century, the British national government began making grants to counties and boroughs to aid in financing schools, local roads, poor relief, and other local projects. Today the device is used in almost all countries.

Defense and Foreign Relations

INTERRELATED FIELDS. All national governments carry on foreign relations and most of them maintain military establishments for national defense. We shall discuss international relations in our concluding chapter. Before we turn to defense activities, though, it may be well to point out how closely these two areas of government activities are related. In the first place, the amount of military preparedness a nation considers it needs depends on international conditions. When it does not see threats to its security and when there appears no likelihood of a major war, a country may keep up only a small military establishment. In times of world tension like the present, all major powers feel compelled to devote the lion's share of their national budgets to defense. In the second place, the bargaining power of a government in international negotiations varies almost directly with its military strength as compared with the strength of the government with which it is dealing.

DEFENSE NEEDS. The defense needs of a particular country depend on a number of factors. One is its relative position in the world. A great power always faces the danger of being involved in trouble anywhere in the world, and must prepare accordingly. If the international situation is such that it is threatened with aggression, it will try to maintain enough military strength to deter aggression. Geographical position is still important, but less so than before the days of air power and long range missiles. So long as the United States could be attacked only by forces carried across a broad ocean, we kept up only a small army, and concentrated on a large navy. Britain, likewise, immune to direct attack because of the English Channel, kept up only a small army but, with an empire scattered over the world, she maintained the world's largest navy. In contrast, many of the countries of continental Europe could be attacked across a land frontier that would be difficult to defend, so these countries maintained large standing armies, but only relatively small navies. The coming first of air power, then of atomic weapons, and finally of intercontinental missiles, has changed the picture drastically. No country is now immune from attack and neither naval vessels nor ground forces, though both are still necessary, can provide defense against an attack by atomic warheads carried by intercontinental missiles. Until the anti-missile missile is perfected — if ever — the only defense against missile attack is deterrence through the power of retaliation. Consequently, a country situated like the United States in its world relations must spend each year, developing these new weapons, an amount of money which, less than a century ago, would have paid all government expenses of the country for several decades.

GOVERNMENT DEFENSE ORGANIZATION. With a few exceptions, the Soviet Union being the most notable, the chief of state is commander-in-chief of the armed forces. If the chief of state is also head of government, as in the case of the American President, he is the supreme commander in fact as well as in form. Where there is a separate head of government, a prime minister or chancellor, that official exercises the real power through his formal advice to the chief of state. There is always at least one cabinet department charged with the management of the non-technical aspects of the military establishment in line with the policies of the head of government. In most countries, there is only one such department, headed by a minister of defense. Great Britain has three: war (the army), admiralty (the navy) and air. In the United States we have the Department of Defense, headed by the Secretary of Defense, but it is divided into three sub-departments, each with a secretary appointed by the President. For the technical military direction of the armed forces, a few countries have established a completely unified command with a top ranking general or admiral directing all the services. In the United States, Britain and several other countries, each branch of the service has its own commander called, in our case, the chief of staff. In the United States the three form a joint coordinating committee, the Joint Chiefs of Staff, with a chairman (another top ranking general or admiral) appointed by the President.

RECRUITMENT. Down through the eighteenth century, the recruitment of soldiers and sailors was everywhere supposed to be on a volunteer basis, though "press gangs" were sometimes used for haphazard drafting when the supply of volunteers was inadequate. The British used such press gangs to keep their navy filled. The French Revolutionists were the first to use a universal draft. During the time of Napoleon, Prussia adopted universal military service, putting each age class of young men through a course of military training, and then graduating them into the reserves. During the nineteenth century, almost all the countries of Western Europe adopted universal military service. During the Civil War, both the Union and the Confederacy resorted to conscription in a very unsystematic fashion, but the experiment was not considered successful. Not until World War I did Britain and the United States adopt systematic conscription, which still fell short of universal service, and Britain has had it ever since. The United States dropped it between world wars, but resumed it on the eve of World War II and it is now routine. After their defeat in World War II, both Germany and Japan were forbidden by their conquerors to have any military forces at all. A decade later, their former enemies, now turned allies, began urging them to rearm, but neither has shown any enthusiasm for it. The small military forces they maintain are recruited only by volunteering.

Church and State

BACKGROUND. In the Middle Ages, church and state were considered equal partners in directing human affairs, though each sought, and in some localities achieved, dominance over the other. With the coming of Protestantism, all sovereign states in Europe established state churches, sometimes Catholic, sometimes Protestant, which were largely under the control of the government. Even the idea of toleration, though advocated by the Quakers and a few others, was repugnant to most people, and complete separation of church and state was not even suggested, except by Roger Williams, the founder of Rhode Island. As time went on, religious toleration became a practical necessity and a demand arose for the disestablishment of state churches.

PROBLEMS. Out of this heritage of the past there have arisen in many countries problems in the relation of church and state and the proper functions of government in matters of religion. Until very recently, very few countries, other than the United States, solved these problems by complete separation of church and state, and even in the United States the issue is sometimes raised as to whether state or federal aid to church schools would violate the principle of separation. In Great Britain, the Church of England (Episcopal) is still the established church in England, and the Kirk of Scotland (Presbyterian), in Scotland. Parliament can legislate on religious matters, but rarely does, so that establishment means only that the clergy of these churches are paid out of taxes. The Church of England was disestablished in Ireland by an act of Parliament in 1869, while Ireland was still a part of the United Kingdom. This law still applies in Northern Ireland. Much later the Church of England was disestablished in Wales. When the Republic of Ireland was created, it was declared to be a secular state, which amounts to separation in that country also. The Lutheran Church is still the established church in the Scandinavian countries and, until Hitler's time, it was also the established church in several of the German *Länder*.

In France, Napoleon Bonaparte made a treaty or concordat with the Papacy which remained in effect until 1905. Under its terms, the government must approve the appointment of bishops but assumed the salaries of the Catholic clergy. During the nineteenth century, there were frequent quarrels over how much control the Catholic Church should have over public education. Finally, in 1905, the French government repudiated Napoleon's concordat, and decreed what amounts to separation of church and state in France. When the unification of Italy was completed in 1870 by the incorporation of Rome into the kingdom, the Pope refused to recognize the loss of his sovereignty over the former Papal States, and an effort to work out an agreement failed. The feud continued until 1929 when Mussolini made a treaty with the Papacy recognizing Vatican City as an independent sovereign state and granting the Catholic Church a privileged position in Italy, especially in matters of education and the holding of property. This arrangement continues under the Italian Republic.

In Spain, Portugal and several countries of Latin America, the Catholic Church is recognized by law as the religion of the nation and is accorded some special privileges. In Mexico, the church-state issue has been critical. In the late 1850's, the Liberals, led by Juarez and Lerdo, gained control of the government. They confiscated the very extensive church lands and abolished the special privileges of the clergy. These laws were not enforced during the long dictatorship of Porfirio Diaz, but the revolution of 1910-1920 went even further. The Constitution of 1917 made all church possessions, including the churches themselves, national property. The church was forbidden to conduct elementary schools. The clergy were not permitted to teach, to vote, to hold office, or even to discuss politics, and the state legislatures were authorized to limit the number of clergy. All clergy were required to register with the government. Little attempt was made to apply these provisions until 1926, when the Archbishop declared he would not recognize them. In reply, the government enacted stringent laws to carry out the constitutional provisions, and the Archbishop retaliated by prohibiting all religious services — something like a medieval interdict. A compromise arrangement was finally worked out under which the laws remain on the books, but the church is permitted to operate with little government interference.

In the old Russian Empire, the Russian Orthodox Church, to which nearly all Russians belonged, was governed by a Holy Synod appointed by the Tsar. When the Communists came into power, they at first tried to destroy religion. During World War II, Stalin gave up the effort and restored something like the old arrangement putting the churches under strict government regulation. These are enough samples to indicate that the church-state relationship is still a problem in many countries.

Suggested Questions for Discussion

1. What are the traditional functions of government? Can you extend the list?
2. Why have national governments come to concern themselves more and more with economic matters?
3. Compare the various theories of the proper functions of government.
4. What are the differences in the meaning of the term "social-

ism" as it is used in: (1) Communist countries, (2) Western Europe and (3) the United States?

5. How far do you think a national government should go in providing welfare services for its citizens?
6. What is the "police power"? What problem has it raised in the United States?
7. In most free enterprise countries, many economic activities are under government regulation. What is the justification for such regulation and how is it carried on?
8. Most governments engage in some economic enterprises. Compare the nature and extent of such government enterprises in various countries.
9. What public service functions are commonly performed by governments? What others are found in some countries? Which ones in each of the major countries?
10. What are "grants-in-aid"? Why are they necessary? How may they become an instrument of central control of local governments?
11. How and why is the relation of church and state a matter of government function in many countries?
12. Formulate and express your own view as to the proper functions of government.

Bibliography

Anderson, R. A., Government and Business (Cincinnati, 1960)

Arnold, T. V., Folklore of Capitalism (New Haven, 1959)

Bianchi, R., Liberalism and Its Critics (Northfield, Minn., 1958)

Burnham, J., The Managerial Revolution (Bloomington, Ind., 1960)

Einaudi, M., *et al.*, Nationalization in France and Italy (Ithaca, 1955)

Grayson, H., Economic Planning Under Free Enterprise (Washington, D. C., 1954)

Hanson, A. H., Public Enterprise and Economic Development (London, 1959)

Hoover, C. B., Economy, Liberty and the State (New York, 1959)

Taylor, O. H., Classical Liberalism, Marxism and the Twentieth Century (Cambridge, Mass., 1960)

Verney, D. V., Public Enterprise in Sweden (Liverpool, 1959)

TEN

Government and World Relations

The World Today

INTERNATIONAL RELATIONS. With the world divided into more than a hundred sovereign states, it is inevitable that there should be international differences and international problems. To some extent, this has always been so. Since the appearance of national states at the beginning of the modern era, governments have given much attention to international relations. They have had disputes and conflicts, sometimes over territory, sometimes over commercial rights, sometimes over disparities in power which enabled one state or group of states to threaten the security of other states. Each has maintained ambassadors at the capitals of other states to try to settle their differences by negotiation. They have negotiated treaties with each other, and sometimes called international conferences. When they could not reach peaceable agreements, they have gone to war. Until World War I, war was considered a normal instrument of national policy. War was not too destructive and usually not too risky.

Today, however, the picture is changed. The horrible destruction of World Wars I and II has impressed upon people everywhere the need to use every means available to avert war. The development of atomic weapons, with supersonic aircraft and intercontinental missiles to deliver an atomic attack, has destroyed the defensibility and security of all countries, including our own. The world situation that has developed, with its constant threat of atomic destruction, has raised the conduct of international relations to an importance that it has never had before.

THE BALANCE OF POWER. The existence of atomic weapons is not the only thing that makes the present world situation different. There has been a complete upset in power relations. For centuries before World War II, there were anywhere from four to six or seven countries that were rated as world powers. Each of these had enough population, economic resources and potential military strength so that it was considered an equal match for any other world power, and far stronger than any country not so rated. These world powers often grouped themselves into alliances to create what was called a balance of power. Each alliance tried to make itself strong enough so that no rival alliance would dare attack it. When one nation or alliance showed aggressive tendencies, a reshuffling of rival alliances or a shifting of diplomatic pressure was often able to convince the would-be aggressor that aggression would be too risky. This did not always work, even among the great powers themselves, and it afforded no protection to a weak state which a great power sought to conquer or dominate unless, as sometimes happened, the other great powers would decide to intervene diplomatically in the belief that if one of their group were permitted to strengthen itself by absorbing weaker neighbors, the balance of power would be upset to their disadvantage. The balance of power idea was the principal basis of diplomatic relations, and in several cases in the eighteenth and nineteenth centuries, efforts to maintain or redress the balance of power caused major wars.

CHANGED POWER RELATIONS. The two world wars destroyed this old power relationship. World War I put Germany out of the great power class only briefly, but it destroyed Austria-Hungary and replaced the Russian Empire with a Soviet Union which, for two decades, was not strong enough to be a major factor in world affairs. It brought the United States recognition as a full scale world power, but in the 1920's we refused to accept the role. Out of World War II, though, there emerged two super world powers, the United States and the Soviet Union. Two of the former great powers, Germany and Japan, were crushed and helpless. The others,

Great Britain, France and Italy, were so weakened that they could scarcely keep their economies alive and would have been incapable of defending themselves against a serious attack, although the United States continued to treat them as great powers.

POLARIZED POWER. This means that effective diplomatic and military power in the world centers around these two giants. Each tries to maintain a balance of power, or more accurately a preponderance of power, by associating with itself a number of smaller and weaker countries. On our side, these are voluntary allies. Some of them agree with most of our aims and policies. Some do not, and were frightened into alliance with us only by the fear of Russia. Each of them has its own interests and international policies, and there are usually points of difference between each of them and the United States. With a few exceptions, this means that they are not fully reliable in a major crisis. On the other side, the nations associated with the Soviet Union are, with the exception of Red China, Russian satellites whose governments and foreign policies are almost completely under the control of Moscow. Outside these polarized camps, there are a large number of "neutralist" or uncommitted nations. These form a majority of all the nations of the world, and this fact is important when votes are taken in the United Nations Assembly. They do not, however, form a "third force" in power relations. Most of them are small, and all of them are weak economically and militarily. Furthermore, they are badly divided among themselves into regional groups with conflicting regional interests. For all practical purposes, power is polarized between the two super powers.

THE COLD WAR. This situation is dangerous. There are no longer other major powers which can keep peace by throwing their diplomatic weight around. Under this condition, it is inevitable that there should be tension and conflict of interest between the two great powers. The ideological conflict between so-called communism and free societies undoubtedly intensifies the difficulty, but it is not the only factor. Probably more significant is the conflict between totalitarian government and responsible government. Most significant is the fact that Russia is aggressive and expansionist, and always has been, seeking to extend her sway over as much of the earth as possible. The only thing new about this is the strength the Soviet Union has available to achieve it. The Communists have just taken up where the Tsars left off. It is to our interest to contain this expansion, just as it was to the interest of Western Europe all during the nineteenth century. The more the Russians expand their power by annexing territory, population and wealth, the greater threat they pose to the security of the whole Free World. Consequently, each side seeks to strengthen its diplomatic and military position in relation to the other, and to checkmate the moves of the other, by every means short of direct armed conflict. This is what has come to be called the cold war.

WORLD POLITICS AND POWER POLITICS. World politics is based on the recognition by governments that developments anywhere in the world may affect their national interests. It is the effort to influence these developments through diplomacy. When carried on by the governments of major powers, world politics becomes power politics. In carrying on power politics, there is always the implicit, if not the explicit, threat to resort to armed force to achieve national aims. Power politics must always operate on the assumption that war is possible (since war is the only court of last resort in a world of sovereign states) so that great powers are always maneuvering for strategic advantage in a possible war. All of the hot spots that have developed in the cold war have grown out of an attempt by one side or the other to gain a strategic advantage. Korea is a case in point. Korea is so situated geographically that possession of all of it by either side in the cold war would constitute a military threat to the other. When, in 1950, it appeared that the United States was abandoning South Korea, the Kremlin decided it was a good time to seize the whole peninsula so, using North Koreans as stooges, they attacked across the 38th parallel. This the United States could not tolerate because, just as in the days of the Japanese war lords, Korea in the hands of Russia was a dagger pointed at the heart of Japan, and we were committed to defend Japan. We were able to carry the United Nations along because the Soviet Union was boycotting the Security Council and so could not cast a veto, but we should have felt compelled to intervene anyway. When General MacArthur pushed north to the Yalu, that was a threat to Russia's territory, so the Soviets threw in the Chinese Communists, who were then still obeying orders from Moscow.

The German situation is similar but more important. A united Germany, aligned with either power bloc, would be a threat to the security of the other. The Berlin crises, which the Russians have stirred up from time to time, are efforts to start a chain of developments which ultimately would bring all of Germany under Soviet domination. Either side will go to the brink of war (over the brink in the case of Korea) to prevent the other from gaining a strategic advantage. Such is the working of power politics.

Diplomacy and Its Machinery

DIPLOMATIC RELATIONS. Most countries of the world maintain diplomatic relations with each other. This means that each country maintains in the capital of almost every other country a representative of its government, called an ambassador or minister. The only difference between an ambassador and a minister is in rank. It was formerly the custom for major powers to accredit ambassadors to each other, but only ministers to less important countries, while the lesser countries sent only ministers. It is becoming increasingly prevalent, however, to give all diplomatic representatives the rank of ambassador. They have staffs that vary in size with the importance of the country they represent and the importance of the country to which they are accredited.

When a new ambassador arrives in a capital he presents his credentials to the chief of state and is formally received. After that, his dealings will be mainly with the foreign minister though, on occasion, he may confer with the head of government. He may sometimes engage in important negotiations, though this is less common than in the days before telecommunications. He transmits messages from his own government and receives messages from the government to which he is accredited. He also gathers information about the country where he is located and sends this information back to his own government. If he offends the government to which he is accredited, that government may request his recall, and this request is never refused.

Occasionally a government may break off diplomatic relations with another government by recalling its own ambassador and sending home the ambassador of the other country. Prior to World War I, such a step was always regarded as the prelude to a declaration of war, but that is no longer true. Breaking off diplomatic relations is now just a gesture of protest against some action which the other government has taken.

DIPLOMATIC RECOGNITION. When a new government comes into power in a country through revolution or other irregular means, all diplomatic relations of that country are severed automatically. It is then within the discretion of the head of government in each country to grant or withhold diplomatic recognition and so restore normal diplomatic relations. In the United States, until about 1900, it was the practice to accord diplomatic recognition to any government that was in actual control of a country, whether we liked it or not and regardless of how it gained control. Now, however, we do what most countries have always done, use the granting or withholding of recognition as a diplomatic device to achieve our international aims.

OTHER DIPLOMATIC DEVICES. Ambassadors in their contact with foreign ministers carry on what is sometimes called routine diplomacy. They maintain normal communications among governments and thresh out minor differences. In the present state of world tension, however, the most important diplomacy is conducted through other devices. Most of these devices are not new, but they are used much more extensively than in earlier times.

SPECIAL CONFERENCES. Since medieval times, special conferences (sometimes called congresses) have been held at the close of wars to work out peace treaties. During the nineteenth and early twentieth centuries, such conferences were called from time to time to resolve a crisis of the moment, or sometimes to deal with some peaceful problem. Since World War II they have become a very important instrument of diplomacy. They are attended by delegations, usually several members each, designated by the head of government of each participating country. These delegations may or may not include high ranking government officials. If the conference is successful, it usually embodies its agreements in a convention or treaty which must be ratified by the participating governments.

FOREIGN MINISTERS' MEETINGS. One form of international conference that looms large in current diplomacy is the foreign ministers' meeting. Such meetings may be held in connection with international organizations on something like a regular schedule or they may be called by a government to grapple with some pressing problem. They have the advantage that the foreign minister, ranking just below the head of government in the management of foreign relations, is in a position to make on-the-spot decisions. Thus, besides rather frequent meetings of the foreign ministers of international organizations, such as NATO, SEATO, the OAS and the British Commonwealth, there have been foreign ministers' meetings of the "Big Four," the United States, Great Britain, France and the Soviet Union, as well as occasional meetings of the foreign ministers of other countries. Much has also been accomplished in bilateral meetings of foreign ministers (those from just two countries) or in a series of such meetings.

SUMMIT CONFERENCES AND PERSONAL DIPLOMACY. Even back in the middle ages, kings sometimes met to make agreements, and during the nineteenth century heads of governments sometimes attended international conferences, but the summit conference as we know it is a product of the second World War. Beginning with bilateral meetings of Roosevelt and Churchill, there were meetings of three heads of governments at Cairo, Teheran, Yalta and Potsdam. There have been innumerable meetings of two heads of governments. One "Big

Four" summit meeting has been held, another cancelled at the last moment, and others projected. By attending summit conferences, heads of government are said to engage in personal diplomacy. It is not the only form of personal diplomacy, though, because heads of governments also carry on direct correspondence. It has become necessary that heads of governments take a direct part in international dealings but, unless it is held only to formalize agreements worked out at a lower diplomatic level, a summit conference can be very risky. Because it is so impressive, its failure can make a bad international situation infinitely worse.

ROVING AMBASSADORS. The roving ambassador or ambassador at large is another useful diplomatic device. A good illustration was the appointment of John Foster Dulles by President Truman to work out a peace treaty with Japan, instead of calling the traditional peace conference. With such diversity of aims and views among the countries at war with Japan, a peace conference would almost surely have become snarled in an almost hopeless wrangle. By going from one capital to another and getting agreement on particular points, Mr. Dulles was able to work out a treaty that was acceptable to all parties concerned. A similar device is the personal representative of the head of government without diplomatic status. Besides being able to confer informally with officials of other governments, such a representative can often go where an accredited diplomat would not be received. For example, he may be able to negotiate a resumption of diplomatic relations that have been broken off.

STATE VISITS. State visits, or formal visits by one chief of state to another, are not usually regarded as diplomacy, but they have a diplomatic motive. Unless both chiefs of state happen also to be heads of government (as when a Latin American president visits the President of the United States) they can not engage in negotiations or even diplomatic conversations. Even so, such visits often help to create a feeling of good will and community of interest that can prepare the way for fruitful negotiations.

Alliances and Other Groupings

ALLIANCES. Alliances have existed from time immemorial, even among primitive tribes. Since the emergence of national states, nations have frequently entered into alliances with each other. Sometimes these are temporary for the duration of a particular war or other emergency. More often, they are to run for a term of years. Usually they do not go beyond promises of each ally to aid the other in case of war. Occasionally they are conditional, coming into effect only in event of a certain contingency, such as one party being attacked by a third power. They are normally embodied in treaties, though sometimes they rest only on executive agreements between heads of governments. During the early twentieth century, some countries joined in an arrangement less formal than an alliance, called an *entente* (French word for understanding). In these cases, the governments involved gave informal assurances that they would stand by each other without making binding commitments. An example was the Triple Entente of pre-World War I days, in which Great Britain, without joining the Dual Alliance of France and Russia, reached understandings with both of these countries.

THE BRITISH COMMONWEALTH. There are several groupings of nations which go beyond mere alliances. One that has the deepest roots in the past is the British Commonwealth of Nations, which grew out of the old British colonial empire. Great Britain has always allowed a considerable degree of self government to those of her colonies that were inhabited mainly by people of European origin. In 1867, Parliament passed the British North America Act, drafted by Canadians, which combined the then existing Canadian provinces into a federal union and gave them almost complete self government in everything except foreign relations and the regulation of external commerce, under the name Dominion of Canada. This came to be known as dominion status. Similar status was accorded later to Australia, New Zealand and South Africa. At the outbreak of World War I, the dominions entered the war individually by action of their own govern-

ments. After the war, they became charter members of the
League of Nations, and some of them began conducting some
of their own foreign relations. Finally, in 1931, Parliament
passed the Statute of Westminster which recognized the
dominions as completely independent nations associated vol-
untarily in a British Commonwealth of Nations. When Ireland
became the Irish Free State in 1921, it was given dominion
status, but when it changed into the Republic of Ireland, it
withdrew from the Commonwealth. In 1961, the Union of
South Africa withdrew. On the other hand, when India,
Pakistan and Ceylon were given their independence, they
elected to join the Commonwealth, and several other former
colonies have done so more recently.

The commonwealth arrangement does not include a formal
alliance. It is rather a cooperative association of nations which
give each other preference in their trade relations and try to
coordinate their foreign policies. The only organizational machinery consists of meetings of ministers. Not only do the
prime ministers meet from time to time to consider general
policy matters, but other ministers meet occasionally to deal
with matters that concern their departments. The Queen is
the symbol of unity. Several of the countries, Canada among
them, recognize her as their titular sovereign. The others
recognize her as Head of the Commonwealth.

THE ORGANIZATION OF AMERICAN STATES. Similar in
some respects to the British Commonwealth, but resting on a
geographical rather than a historical basis, is the Organization
of American States, which includes all the independent nations
of the Western Hemisphere except Canada. It is an outgrowth
of the old Pan-American Union, which was only a loose association of nations which held a conference, the Pan-American
Congress, every five years to discuss common problems. At the
Pan-American Congress of 1938 in Lima, Peru, the nations
agreed to maintain hemispheric solidarity and to join in defending any one which might be attached by a non-American
power. They also agreed that a foreign ministers' meeting
should be called to cope with any hemispheric crisis. Several
such foreign ministers' meetings were held during World War

II. One in Mexico City in 1945 agreed to make the wartime cooperation permanent. Finally, in 1948, at Bogota, Colombia, they drew up a charter for the Organization of American States.

While the OAS, as the Organization of American States is commonly called, seeks cooperation in many fields, including the economic and cultural, it has more the aspect of an alliance than the British Commonwealth. Its primary purpose is the defense of the hemisphere, including defense against communist infiltration. When Fidel Castro turned Cuba into a communist country, Cuba was temporarily excluded from active membership. The OAS has more formal machinery than the British Commonwealth. It has a permanent secretariat and a permanent council of ambassadors in Washington. Foreign ministers' meetings are held from time to time (on call of any member government) and the old Pan-American Congresses are still held at roughly five year intervals.

THE NORTH ATLANTIC TREATY ORGANIZATION. The North Atlantic Treaty Organization, usually called NATO, was formed in 1949, to checkmate Soviet threats of aggression. Besides aiming at cooperation in other fields than defense, it differs from the typical alliance in two major respects. First, it has a permanent council of foreign ministers and defense ministers which meets several times a year. Second, it maintains a permanent joint defense force under a unified command, stationed in West Germany and other strategically critical areas. The fifteen members try to coordinate their foreign policies and to stand together on all issues involved in the cold war.

SOUTHEAST ASIA TREATY ORGANIZATION. The Southeast Asia Treaty Organization (SEATO) was named for its analogy to NATO, but the analogy is not very close. Composed of the United States, Great Britain, France, Australia, New Zealand, Pakistan, Thailand and the Philippines, it was formed in 1955 to check the expansion of Red China into Southeast Asia. Several important East Asian nations are not members. India and Burma declined to join. Australia and New Zealand objected to Japan, and Indonesia was not invited because it appeared to have pro-Communist leanings. SEATO has no joint military force as does NATO. Its members merely promise to consult when any of the Asian members or any other country in Southeast Asia is threatened. There are foreign ministers' meetings from time to time. The organization has not attained the importance or influence of NATO.

CENTRAL TREATY ORGANIZATION. The Middle East Treaty Organization, called the Baghdad Pact group, was organized at Baghdad, Iraq, in 1955. The original members were Great Britain, Turkey, Iraq, Iran and Pakistan. Iraq withdrew after a revolution in 1958, and the name was changed to the Central Treaty Organization, called CENTO. The United States is not a member, but maintains close co-operation. The purpose of the organization, which is mainly an alliance, is to form a military buffer between the Soviet Union and the Near East. It is loosely organized like SEATO, with occasional foreign ministers' meetings, but with no common military force.

THE COMMON MARKET. An organization of an entirely different type is the European Economic Community, usually called the Common Market, composed originally of France, Italy, West Germany, Belgium, the Netherlands and Luxembourg. Growing by steps out of several earlier groupings, this group is in the process of creating a customs union, in which there will be no trade barriers among the members. Eventually they will have identical trade restrictions applying to outside countries. They also look to some political integration, probably culminating eventually in the formation of a federal union. Great Britain and several other European nations are now seeking admission to membership. The United States has given every encouragement to the formation of this group, and is now adjusting its own commercial policies to facilitate trade with the Common Market.

COMMUNIST GROUPS. Until Red China became a rival of Russia for leadership of the Communist world after the death of Stalin, the countries ruled by Communists were all closely tied together under the domination of Russia. Before World War II, the outward manifestation of this unity was the

Communist International, called Comintern for short, which was made up of all the Communist Parties of the world. During the war, Stalin dissolved the Comintern as a conciliatory gesture to his Western allies. After the war, though, it was revived as the International Communist Information Bureau, called the Cominform. This organization still exists, but operates only as a propaganda agency. There was never any question that the foreign policy and military affairs of all Communist ruled countries of Eastern Europe (except Yugoslavia which broke away in 1948) were controlled by Moscow. After West Germany was admitted to NATO, however, delegations from the Soviet Union and all the satellite countries met in Warsaw, Poland, in 1955, and drew up the Warsaw Pact, putting the military unity on a more formal basis. This Warsaw Pact group, formed as a counter move to NATO, is obviously an imitation of the North Atlantic Treaty Organization. Its charter contains exactly the same commitments and provides for a unified military command. It is sometimes called the Red NATO.

The United Nations

THE CONCEPT OF COLLECTIVE SECURITY. As originally conceived, the United Nations was based on the concept of collective security. This means that the peace and security of all nations is to be preserved by providing machinery for consultation and cooperation, and by all governments binding themselves to use this machinery instead of resorting to war. The idea goes back to the Concert of Powers, formed at the time of the overthrow of Napoleon. In that arrangement, all of what were then the great powers of Europe bound themselves to consult in any crisis that threatened the peace, and to take concerted action to preserve peace. The Concert functioned as an organization only for about eight years, but the concept lived on and, on several occasions during the nineteenth and early twentieth centuries, international conferences were held in the name of the Concert of Powers to deal with some crisis.

During World War I, a group of prominent Americans organized a League to Enforce Peace, and spread the idea of a world wide League of Nations. President Wilson was able to get a "covenant" or charter for a League of Nations written into the peace treaties that ended the war. The League was not very different in organization from the present United Nations, but it failed to make a place for itself for several reasons. One reason was that there was never a time when all the major powers were members. The United States never joined. Italy and Japan withdrew when the League condemned their aggressions. Germany was admitted in 1926, but withdrew when Hitler came to power. The Soviet Union was admitted in 1934, but was expelled three years later when the Russians attacked Finland. Another reason for the failure of the League was that the more important countries never made it an important part of their foreign policies and rarely carried their major disputes to the League for settlement. A third factor, growing out of these two, was that the League never acquired the prestige and respect needed to make it a real force in world affairs.

The ideal of collective security was revived during World War II, and it was decided to make a fresh start with a new organization to be called the United Nations. There were several reasons for launching a new organization rather than resurrecting the old League of Nations. One was that the League was discredited by its failure to prevent the war. Another was that, with the greatly changed situation of power relationships, the United States and the Soviet Union would have to be the key members of any international organization that would have a chance of succeeding. National pride would prevent either from seeking membership in an organization which the one had spurned and from which the other had been expelled. Besides, there was a feeling that some of the structural defects of the old League could best be remedied by drafting an entirely new charter. The basic idea, however, was the same: collective security through a world organization.

FORM AND STRUCTURE. The central organ of the United Nations is the General Assembly, to which each member state sends five delegates and five alternates. Each member state has one vote. On important matters, a two-thirds vote is needed; on less important matters, considered procedural, a simple majority suffices. The Assembly can debate and adopt resolutions or recommendations on any international subject placed on its agenda by a member state, by the Security Council or, in some cases, by a non-member state. It adopts the budget and receives reports from all other organs of the United Nations. Although not a parliament, since it has no lawmaking power, the Assembly follows parliamentary procedures. It has a number of standing committees, each member state having a member on each committee. The most important of these is the Political Committee which prepares the agenda for the Assembly. There is also an Interim Committee which can act as the full Assembly between sessions. There is a regular session of the Assembly each year, and special sessions may be called by the Secretary General. Under the "Uniting for Peace" Resolution, adopted in 1950 at the instigation of the United States, the Assembly can recommend collective action against an aggressor if Security Council action is blocked by a veto.

Of almost equal importance is the Security Council. This body consists of one delegate each (with an alternate who can replace him if he is absent) from eleven countries. This delegate is normally the head of his country's permanent mission to the United Nations, and holds the rank of ambassador. Five countries, the United States, the Soviet Union, Great Britain, France and China, are permanent members of the Security Council. The other six are elected by the General Assembly for two-year terms, three expiring each year, and are apportioned among the geographic areas of the world. The Security Council has more power than did the old Council of the League of Nations in that it can order positive action in a crisis which threatens peace. The Charter provided for the creation of a permanent United Nations military force or "police force" to execute such orders. Temporary military forces have been set up in a few instances, such as the Korean conflict, Palestine, and the Congo, but the Security Council has not been able to agree on the creation of a permanent force. Security Council action requires a favorable vote of seven of the eleven members and, except on procedural matters, the seven must include all five of the permanent members. Hence, a negative vote by a permanent member constitutes a veto. The veto is sometimes avoided by a permanent member, which is unwilling to vote for a proposal before the Council, abstaining instead of casting a negative vote.

This arrangement in the Charter was based on two assumptions: first, that the enforcement of Security Council action would require the support of the big powers; second, that the big powers would usually be able to agree on action in any situation that threatened world peace. The development of the cold war and the extensive use of the veto by the Soviet Union have prevented these assumptions from working out. Some people have blamed all the trouble on the existence of the veto. It is well to remember, though, that without the veto, the United States Senate would never have ratified the Charter. In any case, Security Council action against either the United States or the Soviet Union could not be enforced without full scale war — a third world war — and that would defeat the basic purpose of the United Nations.

There is also a Trusteeship Council which supervises the administration of trust territories by the trustee nations until these territories are ready for independence. The Economic and Social Council seeks to improve social and economic conditions throughout the world, especially in underdeveloped countries. It has special commissions on regional economic problems, human rights, status of women, narcotic drugs, and several other subjects. Several years ago, the Human Rights Commission drew up a "Universal Declaration of Human Rights." This document is not binding as law, but at least it sets up ideals which all nations may seek to attain. The Economic and Social Council also supervises the work of the specialized agencies. A number of these are permanent: the International Labor Organization (ILO), the Food and Agricultural Organization (FAO), the United Nations Educational, Scientific and Cultural Organization (UNESCO), the International Civil Aviation Organization (ICAO), the International Bank for Reconstruction and Development (IBRD), the International Monetary Fund (IMF), the World Health Organization (WHO), the Universal Postal Union (UPU), and the International Telecommunication Union (ITU). Temporary agencies have been set up from time to time, such as the United Nations International Children's Fund (UNICEF), the International Refugee Organization (IRO) and the International Trade Organization (ITO). Some of the most beneficial work of the United Nations has been done through these specialized agencies. Membership in these agencies is, to some extent, independent of membership in the United Nations proper. Some U.N. members do not belong to all of the agencies and, in a few cases, nations that were not U.N. members have been admitted to one of the agencies.

Still another United Nations Organ is the International Court of Justice, usually called the World Court, taken over from the old League of Nations. It settles disputes between governments according to the rules of international law when both parties bring a case before it. Some nations have accepted compulsory jurisdiction of the court. This means that, if another nation brings a case against them to the World Court and the Court rules that the case comes within its sphere of authority, they will accept the Court's jurisdiction, appear before it to defend their position, and accept the Court's decision. So far, the United States has not accepted such compulsory jurisdiction. The Court also gives advisory opinions, at the request of other U.N. organs, on what is and what is not legal under international law.

The activities of all of these organs and agencies necessitates a great deal of record keeping, correspondence, and other administrative work. To handle this, there is a Secretariat with several thousand employees, headed by a Secretary General, with an Assistant Secretary General for each branch of activity. A succession of very able Secretaries General has developed that office into a real executive position, directing such U.N. activities as the policing of Palestine and the intervention in the Congo. The Russians have made several attempts to replace the Secretary General with what they call a "troika," or committee of three: a Communist, a Westerner, and a Neutralist, each holding a veto, but so far they have not succeeded. In the view of the Western nations, and most of the newer neutralist countries, such an arrangement would destroy the effectiveness of the United Nations in dealing with trouble spots that threaten the general peace.

ACHIEVEMENTS AND SHORTCOMINGS. The United Nations has many important achievements to its credit, far more than the old League of Nations ever had. The work of most of the specialized agencies has been highly effective in their respective fields of activities. The U.N. finally got the Russians out of Iran, which they refused to evacuate at the close of World War II. This caused the first big clash in the Security Council, but the Russians finally yielded to pressure and withdrew their troops. It has stopped several "brush fire" conflicts, at least temporarily. It brought about a truce between India and Pakistan in their conflict over Kashmir. It achieved a truce in the Palestine War and, while armed clashes between Arabs and Israelis still occur, the U.N. armed patrol in the area has been able to prevent a resumption of full scale war. In the resistance to Red aggression in Korea, the United States bore the brunt, but the operation was under United Nations sponsorship and the United Nations flag. When Great Britain, France and Israel invaded Egypt at the time Nasser seized the Suez Canal, United Nations action brought about their withdrawal. Besides, the U.N. has been able to settle a great many minor disputes, sometimes by negotiation, and sometimes through the World Court. Occasionally a crisis which can not be settled *in* the United Nations can be settled *at* the U.N., which provides an opportunity for unpublicized negotiations between the countries concerned. A case in point was the Berlin blockade of 1948, which the United States countered with the airlift. While the Security Council debated the matter fruitlessly, delegates of the United States and the Soviet Union got together at U.N. headquarters and worked out a settlement. In addition to such specific achievements, the debates in the Assembly and the Security Council serve to arouse and bring to a focus world public opinion, which even the masters of the Kremlin hesitate to defy.

Despite this impressive record of achievement, which is far

from complete, some people are disappointed in the United Nations and can see only its shortcomings. Perhaps these people expected too much. The United Nations is not a magic device that can solve all the world's problems. It is not a supranational government. It is only an instrument of diplomacy among sovereign states. If enough member nations will contribute armed forces, it can sometimes impose its majority decisions on weak states, but it has no means beyond persuasion and diplomatic pressure to compel a great power to obey the decisions of the Security Council or the Assembly. In view of these facts, no one should have expected it to be able to end the cold war, or be surprised that, despite repeated efforts, through special commissions and international conferences, to bring about a reduction of armaments and a ban on nuclear warfare, these problems remain unsolved.

CHANGES AND PROBLEMS. In several ways, the United Nations has changed markedly from what it was when it began operations. The "Uniting for Peace" Resolution shifted the center of activity and authority from the Security Council to the Assembly. Successful intervention in several trouble spots has strengthened the organization generally and elevated the Secretary General into something of an international arbiter. Certainly the prestige of the organization has grown immensely. Probably the greatest change is the one that has come from growth in membership. Almost every independent state (and some that are not fully independent) has sought membership, and nearly all of them have been admitted. About the only country of any importance that has not asked to join is Switzerland, despite the fact that several of the U.N. agencies have their headquarters in the old League of Nations Building in Geneva. The effect has been to destroy the working majority which the anti-Communist nations formerly had in the Assembly. In fact, the new neutralist nations of Asia and Africa, sometimes called the Afro-Asian Bloc, now have a majority of the Assembly votes. It was feared by some people that these states would vote consistently with the Communist group, and so deliver control of the Assembly to the Reds. Fortunately, this has not happened. It has meant, though, that the United States and our major allies have had to revamp their diplomatic policies, both inside and outside the United Nations, to win the favor of these new members. In the long run, this may be for the good of all concerned. The Russians, too, have had to change their tactics. While their cold war opponents had an automatic majority in the Assembly, they could limit their participation to obstructing and trying to create dissension. Now, they also must court the favor of the new members, and so take a more constructive part in the work of the Assembly.

The change in the role of the Secretary General has created problems. We have already noted the efforts of the Russians to substitute a "troika" for the Secretary General so that they could block any administrative action of which they disapproved. Undoubtedly, they will try again. Fortunately most of the new member nations have stood solidly with the Western Powers to prevent this substitution, because they consider the United Nations the best safeguard of their independence.

Another problem is whether or not to recognize the Communist government in mainland China as entitled to China's membership. It is not a matter of admitting Red China. China is a charter member and a permanent member of the Security Council. It is rather a matter of whether the Red regime in Peiping or the Nationalist government in Formosa is the legitimate government of China and so entitled to China's membership. The United States, which does not recognize the Red government diplomatically, has taken the lead in keeping the Communists out, but we have had the support even of those Western Powers, such as Great Britain, which have extended diplomatic recognition. One solution which has been proposed, but has found few backers, is the so-called "Two China" plan. It would turn over China's charter membership, which would include membership in the Security Council, to the Reds, but would accept Formosa as a new member.

THE UNITED NATIONS AND NATIONAL POLICY. Quite in contrast with the old League of Nations, the support and use of the United Nations has become a major part of the foreign policy of almost all national governments. The newer and smaller nations regard the U.N. as the best safeguard of their national independence. It at least gives them world wide recognition and a chance to be heard in a world forum. In many cases, it gives them direct assistance, usually through the specialized agencies, in coping with their problems. Intense in their attitude of anti-colonialism, because most of them have recently emerged from a colonial status, they sometimes make trouble in the Assembly with their demands that some dependency of a European country be given immediate independence, and it often appears that they do not recognize Soviet imperialism for what it really is. They refuse to align themselves with either side in the cold war, and their neutralism can often be irritating. Their great interest in the United Nations, however, stems from the fact that they are not capable of military defense against a big power, and they believe that the United Nations can keep a big power from attacking them. They especially dread a world war, in which they would almost certainly become involved, and they consider that, despite its shortcomings, the United Nations offers the best deterrent to global war.

It is not only the small countries, however, that give the United Nations a prominent place in their foreign policy. The great powers do also. No government lets the United Nations make its foreign policy for it, but they shape their policies in the light of what goes on in the U.N. and utilize its organs to carry out their policies. The large countries all maintain permanent missions at United Nations headquarters, headed by an official with the rank of ambassador. He not only speaks for his country in the Security Council, but is an important policy adviser to his government. As far as they deem it feasible, the big powers utilize the United Nations in carrying out their foreign policies. Sometimes they are criticized for "bypassing" the U.N. For example, many people criticized the United States for not channeling its Marshall Plan aid through the United Nations. A government must decide in each situation whether or not to channel a foreign relations activity through the U.N., being guided by the facts of world politics in each case. In the Marshall Plan situation, where the aim was to restore the economic health and military potential of nations which might join us in the defense of the Free World, to have turned over the administration of the aid to a United Nations organ in which the Soviet Union would not only have participated but would have had a veto, would have defeated the whole purpose. In resisting the aggression against South Korea, it was undoubtedly wise, under the circumstances, to make it a United Nations operation. This was possible only because the Soviet Union was boycotting the Security Council at the moment, and so did not have a delegate there to veto the Council's request that all member nations join in resisting the aggression. The matter could not then have been transferred to the Assembly because the "Uniting for Peace" Resolution had not yet been adopted. However, the facts of power politics were such that, had the Security Council action been blocked by a Russian veto, the United States would have felt compelled to intervene anyway with the help of such nations as might be willing to join us.

It is suspected in some quarters that the Russians would like to see the United Nations dissolved or at least reduced to a mere debating society which could serve as a forum for their propaganda. All the other major powers, though, regard the U.N. as a valuable instrument for holding down world tension and providing a means of international cooperation. It is a part of their national policy to do whatever they can to strengthen the United Nations and to increase the usefulness of the organization.

Suggested Questions for Discussion

1. How has the present world situation intensified the importance of foreign relations for all national governments?
2. What is diplomacy? Describe the regular machinery for carrying it on.
3. Describe some other ways in which diplomacy is carried on.
4. What is the relationship between diplomacy and military power? Why does this relationship exist?
5. What are "world politics" and "power politics"? What are some of the ways in which power politics is carried on?
6. Under what conditions is a "summit conference" likely to

produce good results? What is the danger under other conditions?

7. Describe briefly the principal international organizations (other than the United Nations) to which the United States belongs.
8. Compare the points of likeness and of difference of the Organization of American States and the British Commonwealth of Nations.
9. Describe and evaluate the "Common Market." What is the relationship of the United States to it? What progress has it made to the present time?
10. Describe the structure of the United Nations and tell how it operates. Why has it been more successful than the old League of Nations?
11. Compare the shortcomings and achievements of the United Nations. In what ways, besides specific achievements, has the United Nations proved useful?
12. How does the operation of the United Nations affect the foreign policy of various countries?

Bibliography

Brookings Institution, Changing Environment of International Relations (Washington, D. C., 1956)

Butterfield, H., International Conflict in the Twentieth Century (New York, 1960)

Deniau, J. F., The Common Market (London, 1962)

Goodspeed, S. S., Nature and Functions of International Organization (New York, 1959)

Herz, J. H., International Politics in the Atomic Age (New York, 1962)

Jennings, W., The British Commonwealth of Nations (London, 1962)

Keeton, G. W., The British Commonwealth: the Development of its Laws and Constitutions (London, 1962)

McClelland, C. A., The United Nations: The Continuing Debate (San Francisco, 1960)

McLellan, D. S., and others, Theory and Practice of International Relations (New York, 1959)

Manger, W., Pan America in Crisis (Washington, D. C., 1961)

Morris, R. W., Our Commonwealth in the New World (London, 1960)

Murray, A., Our Changing Commonwealth (London, 1960)
Schleicher, C. P., International Relations: Cooperation and Conflict (Englewood Cliffs, N. J., 1962)
Whitaker, U. G., Propaganda and International Relations (San Francisco, 1960)

General Bibliography

Adams, J. C., and Barile, P., The Government of Republican Italy (Boston, 1961)

Almond, G. A., and Coleman, J. S., Eds., Politics of the Developing Areas (Princeton, 1960)

Andrews, W. G., Ed., European Political Institutions (Princeton, 1962)

Arneson, B. A., The Democratic Monarchies of Scandinavia (New York, 1949)

Baldwin, A. J., Fundamentals of Contemporary Foreign Governments (Latrobe, Pa., 1960)

Beer, S. H., Vlam, A. B., Wahl, N., Spiro, H. J., and Eckstein, H., Patterns of Government (New York, 1962)

Brown, G. W., and Merritt, A. S., Canadians and Their Government (Don Mills, Ontario, 1962)

Carter, G. M., Herz, J. H., and Ranney, J. C., Major Foreign Powers (New York, 1957)

Clokie, H. M., Canadian Government and Politics (New York, 1950)

Derry, K., The United Kingdom (London, 1962)

Dragnich, A. N., Major European Governments (Homewood, Ill., 1961)

Finer, H., Major Governments of Modern Europe (Evanston, Ill., 1959)

Godfrey, E. D., The Government of France [as of 1958] (New York, 1962)

Harrison, W., The Government of Britain (London, 1960)

Hermans, F. A., The Fifth Republic (Notre Dame, Ind., 1960)

Lapence, J. A., The Government of the Fifth Republic (Berkeley, Cal., 1960)

Litchfield, E. H., Ed., Governing Postwar Germany (Ithaca, N. Y., 1953)

McClellan, G. S., Ed., Two Germanies (New York, 1959)

Munro, W. B., and Ayearst, M., The Governments of Europe (New York, 1954)

Neumann, R. G., European and Comparative Government (New York, 1960)

O'Connor, F., Ed., Kings, Lords and Commons (New York, 1959)

Ogg, F. A., English Government and Politics (New York, 1936)

Pollock, J. K., Ed., German Democracy at Work (Ann Arbor, Mich., 1955)

Rappard, W. E., The Government of Switzerland (New York, 1936)

Roucek, J. S., Government and Politics Abroad (New York, 1948)

Rich, C. A. L., Ed., European Politics and Government (Cardiff, Wales, 1962)

Sharabi, H. B., Governments and Politics in the Middle East in the Twentieth Century (Princeton, 1962)

Shotwell, J. T., Ed., Governments of Continental Europe (New York, 1952)

Stewart, M., Modern Forms of Government (New York, 1960)

Wahl, N., The Fifth French Republic (New York, 1959)

Williams, P. M., and Harrison, M., De Gaulle's Republic (London, 1961)

Zink, Harold, Modern Governments (Princeton, 1962)

Thumbnail Sketches of Sixty Governments

Note. The governments of the major powers are not included in this list because they have been described adequately in the text. A number of very small or remote countries are omitted because of their relative unimportance. Most of the newly independent countries of Africa are excluded because they have not yet developed definite forms of government; many of them are operating under provisional dictatorships. Several other countries in the Middle East or Southeast Asia are omitted because they are in the throes of revolutionary change.

AFGHANISTAN, KINGDOM OF. A unitary constitutional monarchy. The bicameral parliament consists of a Senate of 50 members, appointed for life by the sovereign, and a National Assembly of 171 members elected by restricted suffrage. The Prime Minister and Cabinet, appointed by the King, are nominally responsible to the National Assembly, but the King still exercises major executive control.

ALBANIA, PEOPLE'S REPUBLIC OF. Except that it is unitary instead of federal, the Albanian government follows the Soviet model closely. Nominally, supreme power is vested in a unicameral National Assembly which operates through a Presidium when not in session. The Chairman of the Presidium acts as chief of state. The Prime Minister and Cabinet are elected by the Assembly and are responsible to it. The Albanian Labor (Communist) Party maintains complete control through Soviet type elections, so that the Secretary General of the Party, Enver Hoxha, is virtual dictator.

ARGENTINA (THE ARGENTINE REPUBLIC). A quasi-federal republic, modeled on the United States of America. The Federal District (Buenos Aires), like the District of Columbia, is under direct national control. Each of the 22 provinces has its own constitution, with an elected governor and legislature, but in emergencies the President may suspend a provincial government and put the province under a "federal interventor." The President and Vice President are elected by an electoral college for six-year terms. The Vice President presides over the Senate. Congress is bicameral; members of both houses are chosen for six-year terms with one third of each house renewed every two years. The 46 Senators are chosen by the provincial legislatures; members of the Chamber of Deputies are elected by direct popular vote with universal adult suffrage. For nearly half a century prior to 1916, Argentina maintained political stability under her democratic constitution. Since then, the constitutional order has been interrupted several times by dictatorships and military seizures of power.

AUSTRALIA, COMMONWEALTH OF. A federal union of six "states," and member of the British Commonwealth of Nations. The British monarch is recognized as titular sovereign and is represented by a Governor General for the union and a Governor for each state. These are appointed on nomination by the cabinet of the union or the state, and have only the formal duties of a chief of state. Supreme power is exercised by a bicameral Parliament, members of both houses of which are elected by direct popular vote with universal adult suffrage. The 60 Senators are apportioned equally among the states, are elected for six-year terms, and one half are renewed every three years. The 124 members of the House of Representatives are apportioned according to population and are elected for three-year terms, subject to an earlier dissolution. The cabinet system of government follows the British model closely.

AUSTRIA, REPUBLIC OF. A federal union of nine provinces, one of which is the capital city of Vienna. The central government has much greater powers than the provincial governments. The President, a mere ceremonial chief of state, is elected directly for a six-year term. The *Bundesrat* has 50 members chosen by the provincial legislatures. The 165 members of the *Nationalrat* are popularly elected in single member districts for four-year terms. Under a permanent coalition of the two major parties, the Chancellor is the leader of the majority party in the *Nationalrat* and the Cabinet is apportioned between the parties. They are technically responsible to the *Nationalrat* but, because of the coalition arrangement, there is never a no-confidence vote or a dissolution.

BELGIUM, KINGDOM OF. A unitary constitutional monarchy with some autonomy for the nine provinces. The Senate, with limited powers, is elected partly directly and partly indirectly. Members of the Chamber of Deputies are elected directly for four-year terms under proportional representation. Citizens who do not vote are fined. The King, little more than a ceremonial chief of state, appoints the Prime Minister, but must select a party leader who can form a coalition cabinet. Prime Minister and Cabinet are responsible to the Chamber of Deputies and must resign on a no-confidence vote. Dissolutions are possible but rarely occur.

BOLIVIA (THE BOLIVIAN REPUBLIC). A unitary republic with a presidential type of government. The President and members of both houses of Congress are elected directly, Senators for six-year terms, President and Deputies for four-year terms. The Cabinet is appointed by and responsible to the President alone. All persons who have reached the age of 20 can vote. Disturbances of the constitutional order and military dictatorships have been frequent.

BRAZIL, THE UNITED STATES OF. A federal union of 20 "states," with five territories and a federal district. The President is elected directly for a five-year term and may not succeed himself. Senators are elected for eight year terms, Deputies for four-year terms, both under proportional representation. The government is normally of the presidential type, but in 1961 the constitution was amended to transfer most of the executive power to a Prime Minister elected by Congress. Each "state" has its own constitution with an elective governor and a bicameral legislature.

BULGARIA, PEOPLE'S REPUBLIC OF. In most respects, the government follows the Russian pattern. Nominally, supreme power is vested in a unicameral National Assembly whose members are elected for four-year terms by universal suffrage. Voting age is 18. The Assembly elects a Presidium, consisting of a chairman, two vice-chairmen and 15 members, which performs the usual functions of a legislature between the brief meetings of the Assembly. The Chairman of the Presidium acts as chief of state. The Presidium also appoints the ministers, interprets the laws, calls elections, ratifies treaties, and appoints civil, military and diplomatic officials. Actual power is exercised by the Presidium or Politburo of the Communist Party.

BURMA, REPUBLIC OF. A unitary republic with cabinet-type government. Members of both houses of Parliament, the Chamber of Deputies and the Chamber of Nationalities, are elected for four-year terms. The President, a mere ceremonial chief of state, is elected by Parliament. The Prime Minister and Cabinet, formally appointed by the President, are nominated by and are responsible to the Chamber of Deputies.

CANADA, DOMINION OF. A federal union of ten provinces, a member of the British Commonwealth of Nations. The British monarch is recognized as titular sovereign of Canada and is represented by a Governor General (usually a Canadian) appointed on nomination of the Canadian Cabinet. Each province has a Lieutenant Governor appointed on nomination of its own cabinet. Parliament consists of a Senate with very limited powers, whose members are appointed for life, and a House of Commons whose members are apportioned according to population and are elected from single member districts for maximum five-year terms. There is usually a dissolution before the end of the five years. Except Quebec, the provinces have unicameral legislatures. The cabinet-type government, both of the Dominion and of each province, follows the British model very closely.

CEYLON, REPUBLIC OF. A unitary republic, member of the British Commonwealth of Nations. For several years after independence, Ceylon was a dominion with a governor general appointed by the British monarch on nomination of Singhalese Cabinet. The country has now declared itself a republic and substituted an elected president for the governor general. The House of Representatives is popularly elected, but half of the Senators are appointed (by the President on nomination of the Cabinet) and the other half are elected by the House of Representatives. The Prime Minister and Cabinet are responsible to the House of Representatives.

CHILE, REPUBLIC OF. A unitary republic with presidential-type government. The President is elected directly every six years. Senators are elected for eight-year terms, with one half renewed every four years, and Deputies are all elected every four years. All literate Chileans over 21 years of age may vote. The Cabinet is responsible to the President alone. Chile is one of the few Latin American countries where democracy usually works smoothly and disruptions of the constitutional order are rare.

CHINA (NATIONALIST). THE REPUBLIC OF CHINA. Although it claims to be the legitimate government of all China, and is so recognized by the United States, the Nationalist government has actual control only of the Island of Formosa or Taiwan. It appoints the provincial governor of Formosa, but there is an elective provincial legislature. The Nationalist government itself is little more than a skeleton. It consists of the President, who is declared to have supreme power, and five *yuan* or councils. The Executive Yuan, equivalent to a ministry or cabinet, is appointed by and responsible to the President. The Legislative Yuan and the Control Yuan (censorship and internal security) are, according to the constitution, elected for three-year terms, but it has been impossible to hold elections in mainland China. The Judicial Yuan (supreme court) and Examination Yuan (civil service board) are appointed by the President.

CHINA (COMMUNIST). PEOPLE'S REPUBLIC OF CHINA. All power is vested in a Government Council which consists of a chairman (usually referred to as President of the country), six vice chairmen, and 56 members. Actually self-perpetuating, the Government Council is nominally elected by the People's Political Consultative Conference (the nearest thing to a parliament) which represents Communist and collaborating groups. The Government Council appoints the State Administration Council (the Premier and ministries, which are mostly committees), the Military Council, the Supreme Court, and the Procurator General. So far, there has been no pretense of a nationwide election.

COLOMBIA, REPUBLIC OF. A unitary republic, with some autonomy for the provinces. The government is of the presidential type. An amendment adopted in 1957, to operate for 12 years, provides for equal representation of the two major political parties in both houses of Congress, regional legislatures, municipal councils, and most other organs of government. The President, elected directly for a four-year term and not eligible for reelection, alternates between the two parties. The arrangement appears to be working well. All citizens over 21 may vote.

COSTA RICA, REPUBLIC OF. A unitary republic with presidential-type government. The President and members of the unicameral Congress are popularly elected for four-year terms. There is no army. Since 1882, with two brief intervals, Costa Rica has maintained orderly constitutional government. Elections are free and all citizens over 21 may vote.

CUBA, REPUBLIC OF. Before Castro's seizure of power in 1959, Cuba was a unitary republic with a presidential-type of government and a bicameral Congress. True, presidents sometimes turned into dictators, but at least the forms of democratic self government were preserved. Once in control, Castro nullified the constitution by dissolving Congress, filling all government posts with his own followers, and refusing to call an election. Today, he is the government, with the title of Prime Minister. He has set up a puppet President, but that official has no real authority. Castro has declared himself to be a "Marxist-Leninist," and maintains close ties with Moscow.

CZECHOSLOVAKIA (THE CZECHOSLOVAK REPUBLIC). In form, a unitary republic with a cabinet-type government. The Constitution gives supreme power to the unicameral Parliament which elects a President for a seven-year term. The President formally appoints the Prime Minister and Cabinet, but these are responsible to Parliament. Actually, they are selected by the central committee of the Communist Party. By the use of Soviet-type elections, the Communists and a small group of collaborationist parties maintain solid control of Parliament. Between world wars, Czechoslovakia was a true parliamentary democracy.

DENMARK, KINGDOM OF. A unitary constitutional monarchy with cabinet-type government. Both houses of Parliament are chosen according to proportional representation. Members of the lower house are elected directly by voters over 25 years of age. One fourth of each new upper house is chosen by the outgoing upper house; the others are elected indirectly, through electoral colleges, by voters over 35 years of age. The Prime Minister and Cabinet are appointed formally by the King, but they are selected on the basis of a parliamentary majority. They are responsible to the lower house.

DOMINICAN REPUBLIC. A unitary republic with presidential-type government. The President and members of both houses of Congress are elected directly for five-year terms. In certain circumstances, specified in the constitution, the President may rule by decree without congressional action. The country has been afflicted with dictators, such as the late Rafael Trujillo, who sometimes hold the presidency and sometimes install a puppet President, but hold the command of the armed forces.

ECUADOR (REPUBLIC OF THE EQUATOR). A unitary republic with presidential-type government. There is a bicameral Congress. The President is elected for a four-year term and can not be reelected until an intervening term has elapsed. The country has been plagued by military seizures of power.

EGYPT (THE UNITED ARAB REPUBLIC). Virtually a dictatorship, Egypt was formerly a unitary republic with cabinet-type government. In 1954, Gamal Abdel Nasser seized power in a military *coup d'état*. In 1958, Syria was united with Egypt and the name became United Arab Republic. Syria has since seceded, but the name United Arab Republic is retained by Egypt. Nasser has abolished the elective parliament and substituted a "Council of the Nation," whose members he appoints. Political parties are prohibited. The President rules by decree. The ministers are responsible to him alone. Nasser's provisional constitution was approved in a plebiscite.

FINLAND, REPUBLIC OF. A unitary republic with presidential-type government. The President is elected indirectly through an electoral college for a six-year term. He appoints the Cabinet, which is responsible to him. Members of the unicameral Diet are elected for three-year terms by proportional representation.

GREECE, KINGDOM OF. A unitary constitutional monarchy with cabinet-type government. The popularly elected parliament is unicameral. The King is a mere ceremonial chief of state.

HAITI, REPUBLIC OF. A unitary republic with presidential-type government. Senators are elected for six-year terms, Deputies for four-year terms. More often than not, elections have been controlled by a dictator-president. The President is elected nominally by a two-thirds vote of the National Assembly, the two houses of parliament meeting jointly for the purpose. In practice, most presidents have seized power by a *coup d'état* and have then been confirmed by a subservient Assembly.

HONDURAS, REPUBLIC OF. A unitary republic with presidential-type government. The President and members of the unicameral Congress are popularly elected for six-year terms, and the President can not be reelected. The country has been characterized by political instability and internal disorder.

HUNGARY, REPUBLIC OF. Government follows Russian pattern in many respects. Formally, supreme power rests in a National Assembly of 298 members elected from 20 districts on single lists. A presidium exercises the functions of the Assembly between its brief sessions. In form, the Assembly enacts legislation and appoints and dismisses the ministers. The presidium, called the Presidential Council, consists of a President (who also acts as ceremonial chief of state), two vice presidents, and 17 members. The ministers, who are hand picked by the central committee of the Communist Party and can not be members of the Presidential Council, exercise all real power.

ICELAND, REPUBLIC OF. A unitary republic with cabinet-type government. The President, popularly elected for a four-year term, is only ceremonial chief of state. Members of the parliament, called the *Althing*, are elected under proportional representation, without indication of the house in which they are to serve. After the election, the members choose one third of their number as an upper house, the remaining members constituting the lower house. The Prime Minister and Cabinet, appointed formally by the President, are selected on the basis of a parliamentary majority and are responsible to the *Althing*. Elections occur when the Cabinet orders a dissolution of parliament.

INDIA, REPUBLIC OF. A quasi-federal republic of 28 component "states." The "states" are grouped into three classes. Classes A and B have considerable self government with elected legislatures and responsible ministries. Their governors, however, are appointed by the President (on nomination of the Prime Minister) and represent the central government, exercising a number of powers independently of their ministries; they may also reserve local laws for approval of the central government. India is a member of the British Commonwealth of Nations, recognizing the British monarch as "head of the Commonwealth," but not as sovereign of India. The President, a mere ceremonial chief of state, is elected for a five-year term by an electoral college consisting of all members of both houses of the National Parliament and all members of the state legislatures. The upper house of Parliament, called the Council of States, has 250 members who serve for six years, one third retiring every two years. Twelve are appointed by the President in recognition of preeminence in literature, the arts, science or business. The others are elected by an electoral college made up of members of the state legislatures. Members of the lower house, called the House of the People, are elected for five-year terms by universal suffrage. The government is of the cabinet type. The Prime Minister is formally appointed by the President, but is the leader of the political party with a majority in the House of the People. He chooses his own cabinet colleagues on a party basis and they are formally appointed by the President. In time of emergency, the central government may take over the rule of class A and B states. Class C states are governed regularly by representatives of the central government.

INDONESIA, REPUBLIC OF. In form, a unitary republic with a government that is a combination of cabinet and presidential types. Members of the unicameral parliament, called the House of Representatives, are elected under proportional representation for four-year terms. All persons over 18 years of age may vote. The Prime Minister and Cabinet are constitutionally responsible to the House of Representatives. However, the President is permitted by the constitution to dissolve the House, suspend the constitution and govern by decree. President Sukarno has done this so that, for the time being, Indonesia is a dictatorship.

IRAN, KINGDOM OF (*formerly* PERSIA). A unitary constitutional monarchy with cabinet-type government. Members of the lower house of the bicameral parliament are elected. One half of the Senators are elected and the other half are appointed by the Shah. The Prime Minister and Cabinet are responsible to parliament and may request the Shah to dissolve the lower house. The Shah (king) exercises more discretionary power than is usual in parliamentary monarchies.

IRELAND, REPUBLIC OF. A unitary republic with cabinet-type government. The President, a mere ceremonial chief of state, is directly elected for a seven-year term. The Prime Minister, who selects his own Cabinet, is appointed by the President on nomination of the *Dail Eireann* (lower house of Parliament) and is responsible to the *Dail*. He may "advise" the President to dissolve the *Dail* and call an election. Members of the *Dail* are popularly elected under proportional representation for maximum five-year terms. Of the sixty members of the Senate, which has very limited powers, eleven are designated by the Prime Minister, six by the universities, and forty-three by vocational groups. Ireland has withdrawn from the British Commonwealth of Nations, but still enjoys privileged relations with Great Britain.

ISRAEL, REPUBLIC OF. A unitary republic with cabinet-type government. The unicameral parliament, *the Knesset,* elects the President for a five-year term. All citizens over 21 years of age vote for members of the *Knesset.* The Prime Minister and Cabinet, who are responsible to the *Knesset,* are selected on the basis of party strength in parliament and are appointed formally by the President.

JAPAN (NIPPON), EMPIRE OF. A unitary constitutional monarchy with some federal features (the prefectures now elect their own officers and enjoy a large measure of local self-government). The Emperor has been reduced to a mere ceremonial chief of state. Members of the House of Councillors are elected, 100 at large and 150 from the prefectures. The powers of this house are limited in a manner similar to the British House of Lords. Members of the House of Representatives are elected for four-year terms from small multi-member districts in which the voter votes for one candidate only. This provides a semblance of proportional representation. This bicameral Diet or parliament has complete legislative power except that, as in the United States, the Supreme Court can declare its laws unconstitutional. The Diet nominates the Prime Minister (one of its own members) who is formally appointed by the Emperor, and who then selects the members of his own Cabinet, a majority of whom must also be members of one house or other of the Diet. The ministers are jointly responsible to the House of Representatives. On failure to get a vote of confidence, they must either resign or have the Emperor dissolve the House and call an election. All citizens over 20 years of age can vote.

LIBERIA, REPUBLIC OF. A unitary republic with presidential type of government modeled consciously on that of the United States. The President and Vice President are elected directly for initial eight-year terms. They may be reelected indefinitely for four-year terms. Members of the House of Representatives are elected for four years, Senators for six years. Voters must be citizens 21 years of age, belong to the Negro race, and pay a small tax. Some tribal chiefs from the interior are *ex officio* members of the House of Representatives.

LIBYA, KINGDOM OF. A federal constitutional monarchy with three self-governing provinces. Half of the Senators are named by the King, half by the provincial legislatures. Members of the House of Representatives are elected on the basis of one for each 20,000 inhabitants. The Prime Minister and Cabinet are responsible to Parliament.

MEXICO (THE UNITED MEXICAN STATES). A federal republic with presidential type of government. Each of the 29 member states has its own constitution, with elective governor, legislature and courts. The President is elected directly for a six-year term, and may not succeed himself. The Federal Congress is bicameral. The Senators, two from each state and the Federal District, are elected for six-year terms. Members of the lower house are elected for three-year terms. Married men over 18, and women and unmarried men over 21, may vote. Since the revolution of 1910-1920, Mexico has maintained political stability and made great economic progress.

MOROCCO, KINGDOM OF. Instead of an adopted constitution, Morocco has a charter granted by the King. It provides for a Deliberative Assembly, whose members are elected by the rural and municipal councils, which shares legislative power with the King. The rural and municipal councils are popularly elected under a restricted suffrage and have limited powers of local self-government. The King also acts as prime minister, and the ministers are responsible to him alone.

NETHERLANDS, KINGDOM OF. A unitary constitutional monarchy with some traces of its former federal character. The upper house of Parliament, whose members are elected for six-year terms by the provincial assemblies, can not introduce bills or amend those passed by the lower house; it can only approve or reject them. Members of the lower house are elected di-

rectly in single-member districts for four-year terms. The
Premier and Cabinet can not be members of Parliament, but
may speak in either house. They are appointed formally by
the monarch, but are selected on the basis of party strength
in the lower house of Parliament, and are responsible to the
lower house. The provinces have legislative assemblies with
limited power.

NICARAGUA, REPUBLIC OF. A unitary republic with presidential-
type of government. The President and members of both
houses of Congress are elected for six-year terms. Former
Presidents are *ex officio* Senators for life. Seizures of power
by *coup d'état* have occurred on a number of occasions.

NORWAY, KINGDOM OF. A constitutional monarchy with modified cabinet-type government. The parliament, called the
Shorthing, has 150 members elected under proportional representation. On political and financial matters, it meets and
votes as a single body. For other legislative business, it divides
into two houses: the *Lagsthing,* with 38 members, and the
Odelsthing with 112 members. All legislation must originate
in the larger body. If the upper house rejects a bill, it may
be repassed by the lower. If it is then rejected again by the
Lagsthing, the two groups meet as a single body to act on it;
a two-thirds majority is then necessary for passage. The Prime
Minister and Cabinet are selected in the usual way in cabinet-
type governments, and are responsible to the *Shorthing.* They
can not, however, have the King dissolve parliament. Voting
age is 23.

PAKISTAN, REPUBLIC OF. For several years, Pakistan has been
ruled by a dictatorship under a President who seized power
in a military *coup d'état.* He has promised to write a new
constitution and restore constitutional government in the near
future. Under the old constitution there was a unicameral
National Assembly whose members, equally divided between
East and West Pakistan, were popularly elected for five-year
terms. The President was elected for a five-year term by members of the National Assembly and the provincial legislatures.
The government was of the cabinet type, with the Prime

Minister and Cabinet responsible to the National Assembly. East and West Pakistan are nearly equal in population, but differ greatly in area. They are separated by territory of India. Pakistan is a member of the British Commonwealth of Nations.

PANAMA, REPUBLIC OF. A unitary republic with presidential-type government. The President is elected directly for a four-year term and may not succeed himself. The two vice presidents and members of the unicameral National Assembly are also elected directly for four-year terms. All citizens over 21 years of age may vote.

PARAGUAY, REPUBLIC OF. A unitary republic with presidential-type government. The President is elected by direct popular vote for a five-year term. There is an elective Congress or lower house, and a Council of State, whose members are designated by the President. The Cabinet is appointed by the President and is responsible to him alone. The President and Cabinet may legislate by decree, merely informing the Congress and the Council of State of their actions. Most presidents have seized power by *coup d'état* and had their positions confirmed in controlled elections.

PERU, REPUBLIC OF. A unitary republic with a presidential-type government. According to the constitution, the President, two Vice Presidents, and members of both houses of Congress are elected by popular vote for six-year terms. The President may not succeed himself. The Cabinet, though headed by a Prime Minister, is appointed by and responsible to the President. In practice, most presidents have been deposed by military uprisings and new presidents "proclaimed" by the military *junta*.

PHILIPPINES, REPUBLIC OF THE. Except that it is unitary instead of federal, the government of the Philippines is modeled closely on that of the United States. The President, Vice President, and members of both the Senate and the House of Representatives are elected directly under universal adult suffrage. The courts follow the American model closely. As in the United States, the Cabinet is responsible to the Presi-

dent alone and has no direct contact with Congress. The
powers of the President and Congress in relation to each other
are almost exactly the same as in the United States.

POLAND, PEOPLE'S REPUBLIC OF. Government arrangements, in
general, follow the model of the Soviet Union. In form, supreme power is vested in a unicameral assémbly, the *Sejm,*
whose members are elected for four-year terms by the vote of
all citizens over 18 years of age. Soviet-type elections insure
solid Communist control. A Council of State, equivalent to the
Presidium of the Supreme Soviet in the Soviet Union, exercises legislative power between the brief sessions of the *Sejm,*
and its Chairman acts as ceremonial chief of state. The Prime
Minister and other ministers are officially designated by the
Sejm and are responsible to it. In practice, the central committee of the Communist Party dictates to all organs of government. The head of this committee, Wladyslaw Gomulka,
is virtual dictator. He has managed to maintain more independence of Russian control than the rulers of most of the
satellite states.

PORTUGAL (THE PORTUGUESE REPUBLIC). In form, a constitutional republic, but actually a dictatorship under Premier Salazar. The parliament consists of a National Assembly, with
members popularly elected for four-year terms, and a Corpo-
rative Chamber which represents economic groupings. The
Premier, who selects his own Cabinet which is not responsible
to Parliament, is nominally appointed by the President. The
President is elected for a seven-year term by an electoral college which consists of members of both chambers of Parliament and representatives of the metropolitan districts. Salazar
controls all elections by finding devious ways of eliminating
all candidates opposed to his followers. Thus he hand picks
the President, who becomes a mere figurehead and ceremonial
chief of state.

RUMANIA, PEOPLE'S REPUBLIC OF. Rumania has the government
arrangements that are usual in the Russian satellite states.
Nominally, supreme power is vested in a popularly elected
National Assembly, but single candidate elections insure solid

Communist control. The functions of the Assembly are exercised by a Presidium between its brief sessions, and the Chairman of the Presidium acts as ceremonial chief of state. The Prime Minister and Cabinet are formally elected by the Assembly and are technically responsible to it. In reality, though, they are puppets of the central committee of the Communist Party which holds all real power and dictates to all organs of government.

SALVADOR, EL, REPUBLIC OF. A unitary republic with presidential-type government. The constitution provides that the President be elected for a six-year term by direct popular vote and be ineligible to succeed himself, and that members of the unicameral legislature be popularly elected for two-year terms. In practice, the constitution is seldom followed. Most presidents have seized power by military force and been deposed in the same manner. They usually suspend the legislature, along with the constitutional guarantees, and rule as dictators.

SAUDI ARABIA, KINGDOM OF. One of the few remaining absolute monarchies. The King legislates by decree. He appoints the Prime Minister and Council of Ministers, who are responsible to him alone. There is no legislature and there are no elections.

SOUTH AFRICA, REPUBLIC OF. A quasi-federal republic of four provinces. Until 1961, it was a member of the British Commonwealth of Nations under the name of Union of South Africa. It had as its titular chief of state a Governor General representing the British monarch. At that time, it withdrew from the Commonwealth, declared itself a republic, and substituted a President, chosen by the Parliament, for the Governor General. The provinces have their own constitutions and legislatures, but their acts can be overridden by the central government. Government at both levels is of the cabinet type, the ministers being members of Parliament and responsible to it. Formally, the Prime Minister and Cabinet are appointed by the President, but, as in Great Britain, the Prime Minister is the parliamentary leader of the majority party in Parliament and selects his own cabinet colleagues. Members of both houses of the bicameral Parliament are popularly elected by the white citizens; Senators for a maximum ten-year term and members of the House of Assembly for maximum five-year terms. A dissolution of parliament applies to both houses.

SPAIN. Nominally a kingless kingdom, but actually a dictatorship with Fascistic background under Francisco Franco. Franco has the tile of *Caudillo* (leader) and combines the roles of chief of state, prime minister, and head of the Falange Party, the only political party permitted by law. He appoints the Cabinet, which is responsible to him alone. He may legislate by decree. A unicameral *Cortes* or parliament, elected under a restricted suffrage in controlled elections, may formulate legislation, but the *Caudillo* has an absolute veto on its acts. Under a succession law, drafted by Franco and approved in a plebiscite, a Council of the Realm is to be set up at Franco's death or complete incapacity, which is to elect a king, but Franco reserves the right to designate his own successor.

SWEDEN, KINGDOM OF. A unitary constitutional monarchy which a recent King called a "crowned republic." Government is of the cabinet type, with the King a mere ceremonial chief of state. The parliament, called the *Riksdag,* is bicameral, the two houses having essentially the same powers. All standing committees are joint committees of the two houses. The members of the upper house are elected by the provincial assemblies for eight-year terms, rotated so that one eighth are elected each year. The members of the lower house are elected directly under proportional representation for four-year terms. Voters in elections of the provincial assemblies must be 27 years of age and own a small amount of property. All citizens 23 years of age or over may vote in electing members of the lower house. The Prime Minister and Cabinet, appointed formally by the King but selected on the party basis that is usual in cabinet-governed countries, are responsible to both houses of the *Riksdag* equally. However, because of a permanent coalition of the two major parties, Socialist and Agrarian, no-confidence votes forcing a resignation of the Cabinet are rare and dissolutions of parliament, though permissible, never occur.

SWITZERLAND (THE SWISS CONFEDERATION). A true federal union of 25 cantons, each with its own constitution and government. Some of the smaller cantons are direct democracies, with the functions of a legislature performed by a meeting of citizens. Another feature of direct democracy at all levels of government is the initiative and referendum. Members of the Council of States, the upper house of the bicameral parliament, are apportioned two to each canton (like United States Senators) and are elected in such manner and for such terms as the canton constitution provides. Members of the lower chamber, or National Council, are elected under proportional representation for four-year terms. All male citizens over 20 years of age may vote. Switzerland is one of the few remaining countries where women may not vote. The executive is a board of seven members, elected by a joint session of the two chambers after each general election, called the Federal Council. It is not responsible to parliament in the sense of having to resign if no-confidence is voted. It may dissolve the National Council, but almost never does. The Federal Council elects its own chairman, who has the title President of the Swiss Confederation and acts as ceremonial chief of state. He has no individual discretionary powers. The Federal Council apportions ministries among its own members. There is no position that really corresponds to a prime minister.

TUNISIA, REPUBLIC OF. A unitary republic with presidential-type government. The President is popularly elected for a five-year term and may be reelected for two additional terms. The unicameral National Assembly is elected by universal adult suffrage. The President appoints the Cabinet, which is responsible to him alone.

TURKEY, REPUBLIC OF. A unitary republic with cabinet-type government. In 1960, a military *coup d'état* suspended the constitution and set up a provisional regime, but the country is now in the process of returning to constitutional government. According to the constitution, supreme power rests in a unicameral Grand National Assembly whose members are elected for four-year terms by all citizens over 21 years of age. The Assembly elects one of its members as President for a four-year term. The Prime Minister, who is the real chief executive, is appointed by the President and confirmed by the Assembly. He in turn appoints the other ministers who, along with him, are jointly and individually responsible to the Assembly. A Council of State, whose members are designated by the Prime Minister, replaces the Cabinet as the advisory body on matters of general national policy. A "High Tribunal" of fifteen members, drawn from the Court of Cassation (Supreme Court) and the Council of State, may be set up to try impeachments.

URUGUAY, REPUBLIC EAST OF THE. A unitary republic with its government modeled on the Swiss. This little country has long been noted for political, social and economic experimentation. It was one of the first countries to establish bipartisan government on a permanent basis. One of its peculiarities is that it permits a foreigner to become a naturalized Uruguayan citizen without giving up his former citizenship. For many decades, it had elected presidents, but too many of them seized dictatorial power. To end this possibility, the present constitution vests the executive power in a National Council of nine members, six from the majority party and three from the minority party, elected for simultaneous four-year terms by the two houses of Congress meeting in joint session. The Presidency is rotated annually among the majority party members of the Council. As in Switzerland, the President presides over the Council and acts as ceremonial chief of state, but has no individual discretionary powers. The Council members allot the ministries among themselves; there is no separate Cabinet, and the Council is not responsible to Congress in the sense of having to resign if denied a vote of confidence. Members of the Senate and Chamber of Deputies are elected by direct popular vote for four-year terms. Congress appoints a special tribunal of five members to arbitrate disputes between the National Council and Congress.

VENEZUELA, REPUBLIC OF. A unitary republic with presidential-type government. The President is directly elected for a five-year term. He appoints the Cabinet which is responsible to him alone. Members of both houses of Congress are elected directly by universal suffrage. For many decades, the country alternated between periods of dictatorship and disorder. More recently, despite an occasional *coup d'état,* constitutional government appears to be working more smoothly.

YUGOSLAVIA (FEDERAL UNION OF YUGOSLAV REPUBLICS). Officially, a federal republic of six "states," though in practice Communist Party control negates true federalism. Legislative power, in most matters, is vested in a Federal Council of 352 members: 282 elected by universal suffrage, and 70 chosen by the councils of the member "states." On legislation affecting federal relations, these 70 act separately as a Council of Nationalities. There is a second chamber, the Producers Council, representing occupational groups, but its powers are limited. An Executive Council of 37, headed by the President of the Republic, is elected by, and is nominally responsible to, the Federal Council. It has full executive powers. Administration is organized into five secretariats without cabinet status. In practice, President Josip Broz (Tito), as head of the Communist Party, controls all organs of government and so is a virtual dictator. In elections, opposition candidates are permitted, but seldom appear. Although Communist, Tito has been able to achieve independence of Russian control, so that Yugoslavia is not regarded as one of the satellite states.

Index